Clients for whom Keith Bates has applied his Marcom Engine concept have this to say...

From Ed McVaney, Founder/Chairman of J.D. Edwards & Company, which was sold to PeopleSoft – which was then acquired by Oracle. J.D Edwards was a KBA client for three years. "I'd simply like to state that over the three years we worked together it became obvious that Keith is a creative genius with a way of assembling complex product presentations that helped J.D. Edwards increase sales by orders of magnitude." *Ed McVaney, former Chairman J.D. Edwards.*

From Joe Piscopo, founder and CEO of Pansophic Systems, world leader in IBM utility systems for twenty years. Acquired by Computer Associates, Pansophic was a KBA client for five years. "When Pansophic and KBA first began their business relationship Pansophic's marketing needs were immense. Your expertise served us well over the years to quickly and effectively take care of all those needs well. I am grateful for your outstanding professional contributions."

From Oak Stevens, formerly President of KDM Associates, currently Director, KPMG LLP. "Keith is one of those rare breeds of consultants that have always exceeded my expectations. When we were a small unknown systems integrator, his strategy and execution helped to put us on the map and contributed mightily to our being recognized by Systems Integration Magazine as being "best in class" for systems deployment."

From Bob Slaker, Director, World Wide Direct Response Marketing, SPSS Inc., the leader in predictive analytics. Recently acquired by IBM, also a former client of KBA "When we began the process of investigating word-of-mouth marketing and social media as a method to bring our message to new prospects, we turned to Keith Bates to provide a jump-start to our own expertise. As a founding member of WOMMA (Word of Mouth Marketing Association) Keith was able to bring that rare blend of vast experience in tech marketing combined with the latest developments in the fast-changing world of user-driven marketing interactions. Keith is one of my most valuable secret weapons."

EMBEDDED WORD OF MOUTH

Keith Winfield Bates

EMBEDDED WORD OF MOUTH:
How BTOB Marketers use Word of Mouth Marketing in a Marcom Engine to drive quality lead generation

By Keith Winfield Bates

ISBN-13: 978-1461188308

Initial Draft Assembled 2007

Cover and Interior Layout: T.L. Price Freelance • design@tlpricefreelance.com
Cover Image From: fotolia.com

EMBEDDED WORD OF MOUTH

IN A MARCOM ENGINE
drives lead generation

February 4, 2011 BU Today headline
"Facebook Rolls Out Word-of-Mouth Ads"

The social networking behemoth, which boasts more than 500 million members, is rolling out a new word-of-mouth marketing strategy that uses your brand "likes," comments, and location check-ins in advertisements. The approach is called "<u>sponsored story</u>." The ads, which circulate within a member's circle of friends, have already begun appearing on some profile pages.

March 9, 2011 Wall Street Journal
"Facebook Friends Used in Ads"

"Currently, marketers don't have the ability to know or plan word-of-mouth endorsements as part of their campaigns," Mr. Squires said. "This gives a way for marketers to increase the visibility of stories about their organization... "this is word-of-mouth marketing at scale."

Keith Winfield Bates

To Arlene,
whose family was her life, and to our daughters
Cynthia, Dawn, Pamela, and Tiffany

Contents

Preface

Introducing a paradigm shift in the world of technology marketing.

This isn't your father's marketing. That's gone, forever. Dead as the dodo. But the replacement is infinitely more fun, more productive, and can be less expensive...if you do it skillfully. I'm talking about a hybrid. The hybrid that results from blending traditional marketing with word of mouth marketing and its offspring, social media. It's been over 30 years since my introduction to traditional marketing, and only a handful since the world of WOMM (word of mouth marketing) opened up for me. So you can understand that there was a huge bias to overcome. But I did it, and you can do it too if you just develop a receptive mind...and plan on learning a lot. For B2B technology marketers, the payoff will be huge. I guarantee you won't look back.

To quote Andy Sernovitz, CEO and founder of WOMMA (Word Of Mouth Marketing Association), in his opening comments at their first annual conference in the spring of 2005, "There's a sense of history in the air. Can you feel it? You've answered the call to be part of something truly special. There's incredible diversity in this amazing new field, and for the first time, the best and brightest are all together in one place to share and learn from one another." The conference drew over three hundred people from all over the world.

A comment on Viral Marketing. Although you will see occasional references to "viral marketing" in this book, the term "viral" isn't used quite as frequently as it was just a few short years ago. The strategy of viral marketing was initially defined as "managing digitally-augmented word of mouth." And Seth Godin did great justice to the concept in his seminal book on the topic published in 2000, *Unleashing the Ideavirus*. But going viral with a product has as much to do with luck as it does with planning – plus we now have social media making a major contribution to digitally-augmented word of mouth. And then in a category of its own, there's Facebook!

Acknowledgments

First and foremost I would like to acknowledge the tremendous impact of the two books that inspired the concept of the Marcom Engine and thank their authors. *Reengineering the Corporation* was written by Michael Hammer and James Champy, and published in 1993. *Integrated Marketing Communications*, also published in 1993, was written by Don Schultz (who has since become a good friend), Stanley Tannenbaum, and Robert Lauterborn.

Next goes a heartfelt thanks to Andy Sernovitz, founder and CEO of WOMMA (Word of Mouth Marketing Association), for his incredible talents in assembling the key people and the vast repertoire of knowledge that supports the unbelievably fast growth of word of mouth marketing in America. Andy has also become a close friend.

My deepest thanks as well to some of my favorite authors over the years in no particular order: Geoffrey Moore, Seth Godin, Emanuel Rosen, Regis McKenna, Jack Trout and Al Ries, Ernan Roman, Tom Peters, Ayn Rand, Charleen Swansea, David Ogilvy, Napoleon Hill, Robert Ruark, Ernest Hemingway, and Peter Drucker.

And certainly a word of appreciation to all my clients for their patience with me and for the contributions they have made to my learning experiences. Some of the clients who stand out in my memory, again in no particular order: Ed McVaney of J.D. Edwards; Lee Mulder, Joe Piscopo, and Don Landgraf of Pansophic Systems; Bill Lane of General Binding Corporation; Flip Filipowski of DBMS Inc.; Byron Quann and Nancy McCrocklin of IBM; David Sklaver of Wells, Rich & Greene; Pete Dignan of Thumbscan, NETg, and Smartforce; John Haggard of VASCO Data Security; Art Roldan of PCR and Silvon and Novarra; Gary Rippen of Viasoft and Intersolv; and Oak Stevens of KDM and KPMG. There are many others, but unfortunately time has dimmed the memory...but not the gratitude.

A major thank you goes to Al Wasserberger, his company Intellext, and his incredible software invention called Watson which is a desktop search engine on steroids. I owe to Watson a great deal of the success in research for this book, instantly giving me access to relevant information from the web, news, blogs, shopping, desktop, and premium sources...as I'm writing!

Most important of all, however, is the one individual who was most influential in helping this book see the light of day. She is long-time friend and business associate Melissa Giovagnoli, author of the wildly successful Networlding, who acted as my coach and mentor in the development and publishing of this tome.

PART 1

The Marcom Engine

1

What is it?

The Marcom Engine Defined

The Marcom Engine is a systems approach to the process of sales and marketing. It evolved from my experiences as an ad agency CEO/Creative Director as well as a sales/marketing communications consultant for more than 150 technology marketers over the past 30 years. In developing the Marcom Engine, I applied the underlying principles of both Business Process Reengineering (BPR), developed by Michael Hammer and James Champy in their seminal book *Reengineering the Corporation*, and the equally relevant *Integrated Marketing Communications* (IMC) from the book of the same name written by Don Schultz, Stanley Tannenbaum and Robert Lauterborn (both published in 1993).

Quite simply, the Marcom Engine is a database (repository) and a methodology focused on improved business processes to enhance revenue and reduce the dilution of sales and marketing communications dollars. It drives sales and marketing communications to new heights of productivity because it's based on a "best practices" approach.

Enter a Multi-Directional Discipline

The Marcom Engine offers a multi-directional discipline which is your assurance that every facet of your market is being reached with a consistent, focused message and call to action. And it drives revenue enhancement by reducing the waste and inefficiency of the Random Task approach. It consists of six modules: three for planning (audit, strategy, creative), and three for execution (arsenal, deployment, measurement).

Specifically, the Marcom Engine advocates a much greater depth of customer knowledge and involvement than the norm, a unique concept of creative formatting, and the development of a team approach for its implementation. Initially it's more work than the traditional non-integrated process, but it offers benefits that range from simple survival to dramatic growth. My agency has the evidence to prove it works! And once both database and team are up to speed you'll be able to do product launches almost overnight...with major improvements in sales, marketing productivity, and profitability.

If you've ever had that gnawing feeling that half your marcom dollars are wasted...but were unsure which half, or wondered if there really is a correlation between marketing communications and sales or profits, then you need a Marcom Engine. It provides the answers and guarantees true seamless communications to integrate marcom messages, distribution channels, and sales activities, improving cycle times and lead flow by orders of magnitude.

The Marcom Engine Methodology in Action

The process starts with the three **PLANNING MODULES.** These include an AUDIT, both internal and external, of the existing communications environment. Also examined through a complete product analysis are the product's position relative to TALC (Geoffrey

Moore's Technology Adoption Life Cycle), the value proposition, distribution, pricing, and competition. Next is STRATEGY, in which an MDSC (Market Development Strategy Checklist) is designed. This is followed by development of the Communications Support Plan, typically a 25- to 50-page document which evolved from an IBM-developed format. A CREATIVE repository is then developed, incorporating Core Intelligence from the Audit/Strategy modules and Theme/Image standards.

These PLANNING MODULES are then followed up by the **EXECUTION MODULES.** First is the marcom ARSENAL, constructed by drawing from the Theme/Image standards to build a word of mouth, integrated marketing communications tool kit. Elements of the tool kit are then DEPLOYED to fit the disciplines of our media strategy. Following deployment of the marcom arsenal, our strategy assists in MEASURMENT, employing metrics, lead management, and sales support, while monitoring feedback for continuous refinement of strategies. Two measurement disciplines may be considered. The CMO Council's Marketing Performance Management Guide is one, and WOMMA's Measurement Metrics is the other.

Inspired by the Infamous
Random Task Approach

For those of you who may have skipped the Preface, as many people do, the Marcom Engine evolved as my response to the commonly practiced and ineffective Random Task approach to marketing communications. It was common in the 70s – and still is as the 2000s roll along!

You know the routine. Let's try a direct mail campaign. Or let's try running some ads. Maybe an email marketing effort would generate some leads. All we need is a cool website. Webinars seem to work for a lot of people. I think SEO is the answer or maybe SEM if we can get more money. And there's always blogging and podcasting. We don't need ads, we've got good PR. You know the drill: the litany goes on and on. If at first you don't succeed...

By Random Task I refer to the common practice of shooting from the hip, of trying first one medium, then another, endlessly changing creative horses midstream with the hope that something will be productive. If you never apply adequate tools for measurement, you never really know what's working and what's not. Random Task fails to use consistent creative approaches and to support one medium with another. This problem often goes hand and hand with neglecting to apply quality control to creative standards, as well as with unimaginative responses to competitive positioning strategies.

Over the past three decades I have spent a great deal of time counseling senior management and marketing executives on developing more effective communications programs. In the process I have discovered that executive frustration with the frequently poor return on marketing dollars is quite commonly due to a lack of understanding and/or faith in the marketing communications process, coupled with the age-old curse of inadequate accountability.

2 How Do I Build One?

It's easy to get started. You simply fill in the blanks. What's not so easy is the in-depth analysis required to flesh out all the subheads, which will vary a little depending on product and market. This takes serious work—and time. But for the results the effort is worth it. You'll find details of the process in Part 3.

This Simple Chart is Only the Beginning

The chart at the beginning of this chapter contains only the major headings under the six Planning and Execution modules. Where the work begins is in creating and fleshing out the many, many subheads that turn this simple table into a huge, complex chart. Between the end of Chapter 12 and the beginning of Chapter 13 you will find a generic chart that will help you get started. But before long you will discover it needs personalization to fit your situation – so don't hesitate to change it. And keep in mind that this chart only represents the contents of the 25- to 50-page Communications Support Plan (CSP) that follows. This CSP becomes the lifeblood of your sales and

PLANNING			EXECUTION		
AUDITING The Product, the Market, and the Competition	**STRATEGY** The Market Development Checklist	**CREATIVE** Positioning within a system of choices	**ARSENAL** Resources and Materials for Deployment	**DEPLOYING** Word of Mouth Marketing Processes	**MEASURING** Measurement Metrics and ROI Tracking
Primary Market Research	Target Customer	The Process Overview	Traditional & Social Media Collateral	Influencer Relations	Measuring the impact of WOMM
Secondary Market Research	Compelling Reason to Buy	Creative Elements	Marketing Database	Viral Marketing	Marketing Performance Measurement
Communications Audit: External	Whole Product	Copy Platform	Sales Force Automation	Accelerated Contagion	Media Watching
Communications Audit: Internal	Partners and Allies	Theme/Image Standards	Web Analytics	Channel Support	Media Analytics
	Distribution Channels	Market Specific Messaging	Search Engine Optimization	Social Media	
	Pricing		Search Engine Marketing	Experiential Marketing	
	Competition			Event Marketing	
	Positioning				

marketing activities and contains all the information that leads to your development of a strategy, all the words and pictures you've chosen to populate your theme/image repository, all the ambitious milestones that sales are to hit (including lead flow requirements), and lastly a detailed budget to make it all happen.

Successful Applications of the Marcom Engine

User Programmable: The Ultimate Promise of User-Friendly

J.D. Edwards, which was sold to PeopleSoft which was then acquired by Oracle, had a branding challenge on its hands. In the early '90s the company had a low profile in the emerging IBM midrange market, despite its broad range of superb software applications. When JDE came to the Keith Bates Agency for consulting, we launched a marcom effort with a thorough product study based on the Marcom Engine outline. This study revealed that JDE was offering the market something no one else was, but didn't highlight its significance. At a time when software was either sold off the shelf or required expensive modifications, JDE software was designed in such a way that end users could do the mods themselves.

Additionally, intense media analysis suggested that vertical business publications were much more suitable advertising venues than the technology magazines JDE had been targeting (social media hadn't been invented yet). Measurable results for the three-year campaign KBA prepared started at a sales plateau of about $15 million, where the company had been for several years. Over the three years sales leaped 400% to reach approximately $60 million. The Marcom Engine worked. JDE continued the process and became a billion-dollar business.

Industrial Strength Relational DBMS...from IBM

IBM also had a branding challenge, but it was more product-centric than corporate-focused, having to do with their launch of DB2 into the hot (at that time) market for relational DBMS (Data Base Management System). The initial launch of DB2 fizzled for lack of a focused communications effort. IBM was competing with other relational DBMS, including the market-leading Oracle product. Steps that were followed included hiring the Bates agency to refine the marcom strategy. The KBA Marcom Engine would drive the campaign.

After extracting subtle messages from a previously conducted McKinsey study, we positioned IBM's product as the only one offering "industrial strength," a concept which was welcomed by the market and caught on quickly because of the existing perception that only hierarchical DBMS offered heavy lifting. KBA was then appointed to work with Wells Rich and Greene, IBM's agency for corporate communications and software, to develop the creative marketing strategy. Measurable results: as they say, "the rest is history." Today DB2 is considered one of the leading relational DBMS, consistently competing in a duel of giants with Oracle. The Marcom Engine process resulted in an $8 billion increase in software sales,[1] with sales eventually exceeding $20 billion.

---

[1] Precise percentage of increase proprietary

3 Where does WOMM fit in?

Now that we've discussed the traditional approaches to marketing, it's time to innovate. You have the skeleton of a Marcom Engine sitting on your desk, or perhaps in your computer. Where does the paradigm shift known as "word of mouth marketing" fit in? WOMM plugs into those areas of the Marcom Engine chart shown in boldface type and underlined on the next page. Explanations follow:

Word of Mouth Within the
CREATIVE Module

Creative Elements: When developing the creative module for a WOMM/integrated marcom effort, care must be taken regarding the fit of the creative module to the media planned for its deployment. Example: graphics that would lend themselves to a powerful trade show booth may not lend themselves to email or podcasts. Before the advent of the internet and the popularity of WOMM, traditional BtoB integrated marketing communications programs consisted primarily of such media as print advertising, direct mail, and

PLANNING			**EXECUTION**		
AUDITING The Product, the Market, and the Competition	**STRATEGY** The Market Development Checklist	**CREATIVE** Positioning within a system of choices	**ARSENAL** Resources and Materials for Deployment	**DEPLOYING** Word of Mouth Marketing Processes	**MEASURING** Measurement Metrics and ROI Tracking
Primary Market Research	Target Customer	The Process Overview	Traditional Media	**Influencer Relations**	**Measuring the impact of WOMM**
Secondary Market Research	Compelling Reason to Buy	**Creative Elements**	**Social Media**	**Viral Marketing**	Marketing Performance Measurement
Communications Audit: External	Whole Product	Copy Platform	**Collateral**	**Accelerated Contagion**	**Media Watching**
Communications Audit: Internal	Partners and Allies	Theme/Image Standards	Marketing Database	**Channel Support**	**Media Analytics**
	Distribution Channels	Market Specific Messaging	Sales Force Automation	**Social Media**	
	Pricing		Web Analytics	Experiential Marketing	
	Competition		Search Engine Optimization	Event Marketing	
	Positioning		Search Engine Marketing		

telemarketing. Today a plethora of both offline and online media, each with its own requirements, can be mind-boggling. For some insights into this mix, fast forward about five paragraphs to the section labeled Accelerated Contagion.

Influencer relations, traditional PR, evangelism, newsletters, blogging, podcasting, and social media each call for copywriting/content development, but each requires a different writing approach. Video marketing calls for movie scripting, storyboarding skills, and an ability to select footage and sound tracks that reinforce all the written messaging conveyed through other media. Writing for sales support collateral is another world, but must be consistent with all other media campaigns if we are to speak with one voice. And social media content writing is yet another sphere of expertise.

Word of Mouth within the ARSENAL Module

Collateral: When creating collateral – whether white papers, eBooks, testimonials, case studies, corporate brochures, trade show handouts, webinars, etc. – it is important to be sure that the copy and appearance are consistent with messaging being distributed to the company's database of influencers, and that it share the excitement of any videos in production. There are often very different people and personalities involved in putting out the word, but the message has to be consistent whether delivered by the CEO to a key influencer, a salesperson to a prospect, or a marketing exec to a channel partner. The amount of cooperation required to be effective is often intimidating. The strategies presented in this book will help you approach the challenge.

Marketing Database (development and management): The old days of simply buying a list of advertising targets from a publication or list broker are not really gone, but such lists are definitely playing a smaller role. One of the more challenging tasks in the development of a WOMM program is the selection of the influencers. These people are typically dug out of a dozen market segments, analyzed for their capabilities, and managed on a one-to-one basis. The magic number typically recommended for this list is 100, and some professional firms contend that it takes thousands of dollars of staff time to locate and nurture these people using Twitter or other media. This is a serious list investment, often requiring fairly sophisticated portals or dashboards to manage influencers. Many companies specialize in the management of these complex lists.

Word of Mouth within the DEPLOYMENT Module

Influencer Relations: The deployment of messaging when working within a WOMM environment is tricky because it now has two major components. Traditional PR or Buzz is still necessary, and typically consists of communicating with media, analysts, and industry gurus. But maintaining regular communications with up to 100 influencers across over a dozen market segments that impact your business is complex and time-consuming.

Viral Marketing: The creation and deployment of viral messaging is unpredictable and involves the seeding of a variety of mediums ranging from standard email to blogs to newsgroups to communication with trade associations and influencers. Each needs a different carrier message.

Accelerated Contagion: Unlike the simple 90-Day Blitz of yesterday, today's messaging must lend itself to websites, microsites (to augment the main site for niche marketing), blogs, newsletters, forums, email, voice and fax broadcasting, telemarketing, direct mail, tradeshows, webinars, print media, broadcast media and podcasting, experiential, seeding, and social media with its endless permutations. With all web-based media, attention to search engine optimization (SEO) as well as search engine marketing (SEM) is key.

Channel Support: You will often find yourself playing second fiddle to channel support groups, partners, allies, distributors, and others who have a vested interest in selling your product or service. However, your sales are not their highest priority. If order to develop effective materials for them you must understand their positioning strategy and then tailor material to fit that, without giving up your own positioning strategy on which all your marcom is based.

PART 2

Word of Mouth Marketing

4 An Overview

S o much has been written by so many skillful, knowledgeable people on the subject of word of mouth marketing over the past five years that any attempt to sum up all the work in one chapter would be impossible, if not ludicrous. This is not a book on word of mouth marketing. It's a book on *embedding* word of mouth. It is a book on *how to fold word of mouth marketing into the traditional mainstream of marketing communications* so that both benefit, and we are treated to another example of one plus one equaling three.

My books on word of mouth marketing occupy two feet of space on my credenza, and even this collection is dwarfed by the vast numbers published each year. Rather than attempt an exhaustive survey of the myriad important volumes available, I will confine myself to recommending a few of my personal favorites. For those readers new to the field as well as for the old pros who may have simply missed some of these titles, I hope this overview will prove helpful. My apologies in advance to the authors I may have missed.

Leading the pack on word of mouth marketing is Malcolm Gladwell's *Tipping Point.* In the order I was exposed to them, I also recommend *Unleashing the Ideavirus* by Seth Godin, *The Anatomy of Buzz* by Emanuel Rosen, *The Secrets of Word of Mouth Marketing* by George Silverman, *Creating Customer Evangelists* by Ben McConnell and Jackie Huba, *The Influentials* by Ed Keller and Jon Berry, *BuzzMarketing* by Mark Hughes, *PyroMarketing* by Greg Stielstra, *Connected Marketing* by Justin Kirby and Paul Marsden, and most recently *Word of Mouth Marketing* by my friend Andy Sernovitz, founder and past CEO of WOMMA (Word of Mouth Marketing Association), reachable at www.womma.org.

Awareness of word of mouth marketing (WOMM) is growing exponentially in the press and in the marketplace, and yet its application is often poorly understood. The goal of this chapter is to help you understand the process well enough to know where to turn for help, or how to launch your own program.

Word of Mouth Marketing Defined

For the purpose of this book I am dividing word of mouth marketing into three related categories: word of mouth proper (abbreviated WOMM), viral marketing, and buzz. These categories are based on the means through which the message spreads.

In its archetypical form, word of mouth leverages social networks. People talk among their peers, trading opinions and impressions of a new product. This is what we mean by word of mouth proper, or WOMM. Viral marketing, on the other hand, is specific to a message conveyed through digital networks, while buzz marketing leverages media networks.

In the past these categories could be neatly differentiated: word of mouth proper meant face-to-face, phone, or email communication among groups of acquaintances. Today, however, Facebook and Twitter have widened the scope and reach of such conversations, so the boundary between personal communication and media is blurred. Digital networks are inextricably linked with social networks, as blog readers use the Facebook "Like" button to express their opinions to their friends.

Rather than hard and fast distinctions, the categories of WOMM, viral, and buzz represent nuances in word of mouth marketing. Dr. Paul Marsden of VBMA goes so far as to say that WOMM/Viral/Buzz are all the same thing, namely network-enhanced word of mouth. While the extent of interconnection is undeniable, it is helpful from a procedural standpoint to maintain separate categories. Viral marketing, for example, can spread using either an ideavirus or a shockvirus approach, discussed in detail in later in this chapter. Social networking is typically managed through influencer relations. There is no limit on possible distribution vehicles, but it is important to choose a means of dissemination appropriate to the product and marketing strategy.

Viral Marketing: The Revolution That Became a Trend

Viral marketing was first to cause a word-of-mouth revolution. The term was coined by the VC firm Draper Fisher Jurvetson in 1995 to describe the phenomenon of Hotmail, which grew with the rapidity of a cold virus, from 0 to 12 million subscribers in eighteen months. 'Viral marketing' was pronounced marketing buzzword of the year for 1998. From this beginning the concept quickly grew, perpetuating similar revolutions which gave rise to buzz marketing and WOMM. 'Word-of-mouth on steroids,' 'evangelism,' 'influencer relationship marketing' – the variety of terms in use speaks for the widespread currency of the idea. You might say that viral marketing itself went viral!

The phenomenon of viral marketing comes in two forms, described simply for the moment as Level I–Self Perpetuating (purely viral), and Level II–Needs Coaxing (viral with accelerated contagion).

In order to be put in motion, viral marketing obviously requires a virus-worthy or at least newsworthy product or service. The required degree of newsworthiness, which determines whether we are looking at a Level I or a Level II situation, will be reviewed later in this book (see Part II).

Despite its power, it is important to remember that viral marketing, and by extension word of mouth as a whole, is not a standalone tool. Word of mouth in any form must be intelligently incorporated into a complete product scheme. Justin Kirby, Managing Director of DMC, Ltd, has this to say: "In fact the most successful use of online viral marketing is not as a standalone tactic but as an integrated part of a brand's overall marketing strategy. One of the big mistakes brands make is thinking that an online viral campaign is an end in itself rather than recognizing that it's a means to an end. Viral marketing, like PR, is a process not an event. Its point is to create a buzz in order to help build brand and shift product, not just to create a buzz full stop. There is no point in 'attempting to go viral' without fulfilling a wider or longer-term strategic purpose."

Who Will Spread the Word?

Now that we have outlined the various mediums through which word-of-mouth messages can spread, we need to address the question of who will do the spreading. Simply citing satisfied or even ecstatic users is an inadequate answer. They need to be people with a unique set of characteristics.

How do we define these people who put word of mouth to work, who can be depended on to put our message into motion? This is where the terminology gets tricky. Because the concept gained momentum so rapidly, a bewildering array of jargon has been spawned. In this section, I summarize how the authors of the books recommended above have contributed to our understanding of a network's arrangement and functioning. Each author highlights a different aspect, and by putting them together we can gain some perspective on the types of people spreading messages by word of mouth. To build an effective knowledge of word-of-mouth marketing, I encourage you to read one or more of the books introduced in this chapter. The following should help orient you to the notions involved.

The best starting point is to consider the structure of the network which will spread our message. Beyond the mere presence of connections, networks are typified by the varieties of people constituting nodes. Some are highly connected, spreading short messages frequently, while others transmit more substantive messages through fewer connections. The range of possible network users is immense.

Classifying network users according to their role, Malcolm Gladwell's *The Tipping Point* identifies three kinds of participant in spreading a message. The Mavens function as data banks, providing the message at the outset. Subsequently Connectors act as social glue by spreading the message. Finally, the Salesmen or Persuaders reinforce the message when we are unconvinced of what we hear from the Mavens or Connectors. These three types of people are connected both to network hubs, such as smaller industry bloggers, and to larger mega-hubs centered on members of the press, celebrities, pundits, and politicians.

A network user's position is correlated with his or her personality, as pointed out in the book *Buzz* by Marian Salzman, Ira Matahia, and Ann O'Reilly, all of Euro RSCG Worldwide. Mavens (called Alphas in *Buzz*) are powerful influencers, not because of the money they spend but because of the weight of their influence. They are typically independent, confident, opinionated, and curious. Mavens/Alphas are driven by a hunger for stimulation, a disregard for convention, and an urge to take risks. But they are not particularly super-social. Spreading the word in crowds and at group gatherings is left to the Bees (Gladwell's Connectors).

Connectors/Bees are highly connected and communicative, and translate the Maven/Alpha's ideas into usable, digestible data for the mainstream. They are the conduits through which information reaches the masses. Connectors/Bees create "tipping points," and are driven by a love of communicating and sharing with others, a sense of style based on imitation, and a need for confirmation.

As well as the structure of a network and the character of its participants, we must also consider the mechanism by which ideas are spread. To describe the ways in which different users transmit a message, Seth Godin builds on the analogy of viruses and contagion. In *Unleashing the Ideavirus*, he introduces the concept of Sneezers, the driving force behind an ideavirus. In fact Sneezers are so important that they must be subdivided into Promiscuous Sneezers and Powerful Sneezers. Promiscuous Sneezers are members of a hive who can be depended on to pass along ideas that appeal to them. Promiscuous sneezers can be persuaded to perform. They can be bought. And they are seldom highly regarded by opinion leaders, but when promiscuous enough, they are very effective. Powerful sneezers, on the other hand, are discriminating, sneezing forcefully in specific directions. They can't be bought, or their power diminishes.

We can turn all this analysis to our advantage by developing strategies based on our understanding of a network's structure, culture, and mode of communication. George Silverman's book *The Secrets of Word-of-Mouth Marketing* constructs a Decision Matrix to position the right message in front of the right people at the right time (syncrographics). Delivering the message falls to three categories of interactions: expert to expert, expert to peer, peer to peer (in Gladwell's terms, roughly Maven to Maven, Maven to Connector, Connector to Connector). To pinpoint precisely where the message should be targeted at each stage, Silverman adapts the Technology Adoption Life Cycle from Geoffrey Moore's *Crossing the Chasm* to subdivide network users further as Innovators, Early Adopters, Middle Majority, Late Majority, and Laggards. These distinctions inform the positioning of the message.

One of the most challenging tasks in word-of-mouth marketing is reaching network hubs – the regular non-media people who are nevertheless influential in spreading ideas within their community. When found and persuaded, however, network hubs are allies of huge long-term value. In *The Anatomy of Buzz*, Emanuel Rosen calculates that for the example of a car dealership, the messages spread by one network hub might translate into more than $40,000 of yearly revenue, not including the hub's own purchases. When truly thrilled with your product, a network hub might even become what Ben McConnell and Jackie Huba call an Evangelist in their book *Creating Customer Evangelists*. Effective word of mouth marketing can build your company's best customers into these influential, loyal, and enthusiastic promoters.

Finding the Hubs

How do we sort the network hubs out from the crowd so as to put our viral marketing strategy into play? How do we locate the Mavens and Connectors who are critical to our little piece of the world? And how do we determine whether our viral approach should be a Level I or a Level II? Who's going to help us get the job done? Let's explore the options.

Communications companies or consultants are often the starting point unless you plan on doing it yourself, in which case you are in for a lot of reading. Most people won't opt to go it alone as simply being too time consuming. Communications companies include ad agencies (more accurately interactive ad agencies who typically perform viral and accelerated contagion campaigns) as well as PR firms who are typically more adept at influencer relations. All these players have reengineered an old process known as advertising and public relations into this new/old thing called word of mouth marketing. The internet separates the new from the old.

Once you have identified your influencers (mavens and connectors), you can chase them by shooting from the hip, using sales force input and secondary research against in-house developed criteria, or you can employ online, primary research through companies like the Keller Fay Group.

If you're going to do it yourself be aware that the criterion for the selection process is where it gets tricky. There probably are no clearly defined parameters for either the segment auditing or the environmental blueprint for your particular influencers. On the Ketchum IRM website are some examples for one of their clients, a consumer-electronics company. For them IRM identified the buyer/ key target, ultimate influencers, determined detractors, and initial influencers – broken down into a subset of ten specific influencer targets.

The beauty of the influencer database is that is tends to be small and easily (economically) managed. Fortunately for us, 10% of the world influences 90%.

BtoB/technology may not demand the heavy sophistication of consumer research simply because the numbers are smaller, but don't be fooled into thinking that careful analysis is not just as important, because individual sales are typically dramatically greater.

Metcalfe's law, the power behind viral marketing

Metcalfe's law tells us that the marketing value of a network increases with the square of the number of people using it. So when you have 10 users in the world, that's 25 times better than when there were two. And at 100 users your network is 100 times better than at 10. With 100 user hubs who are each connected to 100 more people, your network has a reach of 10,000 people. 100 hubs seems to be the magic number for going viral.

Benefits of employing WOMM

Perhaps the first issue to resolve, because of the nature of the audience for this book (which is primarily B2B technology marketers), is whether WOMM lends itself better to consumer marketing or business to business. The answer is "both" equally well. In the BtoB world it is particularly well suited to the pharmaceutical and technology industries because of the need for one-on-one conversation about technical aspects.

From the customer's point of view word of mouth emanates from a trusted source, is credible, friendly, and tuned to the listener's personal interests. It also overcomes the four most feared words in advertising, "I don't believe you."

Word of Mouth Marketing Takes Many Forms

From Stanley Arnold's *Tale of a Blue Horse* to the incredible stories of Hotmail, Post-it Notes, and a dozen others, you'll find inspiring success stories of WOMM. Netscape, Napster, Trivial Pursuit, and BullGuard software security all offer exciting examples of WOMM.

Choose the approach that best fits your needs. There are three possible approaches, and they range from Ideaviruses to Shockviruses to Influencers.

Ideaviruses spread the word based on a superior product. Shockviruses spread the word based on superior advertising. And Influencers spread the word either through evangelists or through the mavens and connectors in communication with network hubs. These network users are persuaded to spread the word either because of their own enthusiasm for the product or due to corporate-sponsored relationships.

A point of clarification contributed by Justin Kirby: "What's the difference between Viral Advertising and Viral Marketing? Well, any viral advertising campaign is doing viral marketing but what is specific about viral advertising is the use of creative agents rather than the amplification and acceleration of product recommendations." And referencing a recent Marketing Sherpa report, "The reason you focus on the creative agents is because the product normally doesn't have a uniqueness that can be leveraged to amplify and accelerate word of mouth. So you make the creative agent/communications *sticky* because the product *isn't* necessarily."

Challenges to implementation

Both word of mouth and viral marketing are often a tough sell to management because it reflects a major change in the status quo. Budgeting for ads, direct mail, and websites is done every day. But word of mouth marketing? What's that? It wasn't invented in this company.

However, viral marketing can solve some BIG marketing problems. Like achieving quarterly revenue goals. Increasing the numbers of qualified leads. Shortening of selling cycles. Reducing the overall costs of marketing. And inspiring employee and vendor evangelism.

Word of Mouth Defined by the Experts

High tech's greatest marketing guru Regis McKenna explains the difference between word of mouth and all other forms of communication as follows: "It is an experienced process, rather than an observed one. The message is tuned to the individual listener. The credibility of the speaker carries over to the message immediately. Experts can be used in this medium without the negative effect of commercializing his or her position and message. Efficiency... while taking time to disseminate the message, is delivered directly to those who must use the information and act on it. Feedback is instantaneous."

To quote Emanuel Rosen's The Anatomy of Buzz, "To create buzz and use it effectively, you should have a realistic view of the phenomenon, not glorify it. For example, some word-of-mouth enthusiasts argue that if you get good buzz, you don't need to do any marketing. This can be a major mistake. Distribution, advertising, promotions and other traditional marketing activities can translate the goodwill surrounding your product into sales. Good buzz is the best thing you could wish for, but it's just one component of your marketing mix."

Benefits to Marketers *and* Buyers

The simplest reason for choosing word of mouth marketing over traditional advertising is that it can be FASTER, CHEAPER, BETTER! But no guarantees! A study by advertising giant Euro RSCG Worldwide a few years ago found that for generating excitement about products, word of mouth is 10 times more effective than TV or print ads. If you can achieve focus on your product's virus-worthiness, viral marketing will deliver 10X the market impact at $1/10^{th}$ the cost. Viral marketing turns your ideas into epidemics by helping your customers do the marketing for you.

Why the viral marketing approach to word of mouth? In a nutshell it's the speed and low-cost distribution enabled by the internet. And because traditional advertising is costly as well as lacking in productivity and credibility, word of mouth marketing is becoming the best way to launch a brand. Today the speed of information diffusion enabled by the internet is weakening the ability of *marketers* to communicate with customers and strengthening the ability of *customers* to communicate with customers. In other words, it is a dialogue rather than a monologue.

Word Of Mouth Stories and Case Studies

Word of mouth marketing is not really new. From Stanley Arnold's *Tale of the Blue Horse*, published in 1968, comes the story of how United Airlines used word of mouth to inspire executive secretaries to choose United over competitors when charged by their bosses to book a flight. At that time United's public image seemed to lack something. Arnold's suggestion: send a freshly cut long-stemmed rose every Monday of every week for a year to the executive secretaries of the top 1000 CEOs (fifty-two thousand roses). Plus a bud vase with the first mailing. The result: doors previously closed to United salesmen were suddenly open. Within six months dramatic increases in ticketing occurred.

The title story of *Tale of the Blue Horse* is about an imaginative idea General Foods's ad agency, Young and Rubicam, developed to announce a new product to their salesmen. The role of the salesmen was to sit down with the buying committees of retail stores and try to persuade them that a demand for their new products would be sweeping the nation via word of mouth. To help General Foods introduce a new drink to its sales force with flair and confidence, Y&R turned to Stanley Arnold, who dreamed up the idea of a blue horse representing General Foods's promise that the new product line would definitely be "a horse of a different color."

On meeting day the blue horse had been tethered to a tree about forty feet from the bar. After the first round of drinks the salesmen of General Foods could not believe their eyes. "These drinks are so damn good, one of the regional sales managers said to me, I believe I see a blue horse out there." All the others said the same thing, but none could believe what their eyes told them.

Finally the meeting began as General Foods announced to its salesmen that their company was going to give them the most exciting line of products in their company's glorious history. General Foods revealed it was going into gourmet foods. Everyone quickly had a second drink. At first the applause was perfunctory. Some of it even sounded like hissing.

"This is new territory for General Foods," the speaker went on. "You might even say that compared to what you've been selling until now, this is a horse of a different color."

At that point they responded. They had seen a blue horse out there. Now they knew what it was all about. The meeting finally picked up momentum, and to the extent that experienced food salesmen can summon up enthusiasm for gourmet foods, these salesmen were close to a level of exuberance. The introduction of the gourmet line was dispatched beyond anyone's expectations.

Then the Internet Arrived

The Hotmail story started in 1995 with two young men from Silicon Valley, each working for a different company, but needing to collaborate on a common project without using their company's email. Suddenly they had a bright idea: a free email service that could be accessed through the web. With only $300,000 in VC seed money they launched the company. A word of mouth program conveyed both electronically and face-to-face started to spread the word. It was good old word of mouth marketing at internet speed. Within two months they had 100,000 users, and by eighteen months they had 12 million subscribers. The term 'viral marketing' evolved from this success story. Microsoft bought Hotmail for $400 million and as of 2001 was signing up a hundred thousand people a day.

Napster, a way of networking people's hard drives so that they can share music, spread so fast in only a few months that it threatened the entire recording industry and appeared on the cover of Newsweek!

The story of Post-It notes is so good it ought to be apocryphal, but it's actually true. Nobody was buying the product. 3M was going to cancel the whole program. Then the brand manager of the product persuaded the secretary of 3M's chairman to send a case of Post-Its to the secretaries of the chairmen of the other 499 Fortune 500 Companies. Suddenly, the most powerful sneezers in the most powerful companies in the country were sending around memos, all in the form of comments scrawled on Post-Its. It took just a few months after that for it to become yet another successful business communication device. A classic ideavirus.

And now, a case study compliments of WOMMA, taken from their book 2011 WORD OF MOUTH WORKS, award-winning examples of effective word of mouth marketing campaigns.

Eloqua/Eloqua
Silver Medal Winner of Momentum Award 2011

Business Problem

Founded over a decade ago, Eloqua created the marketing automation category and established itself as the provider of choice for more than 50,000 marketers across 35 countries. However, its core technology was basically the same in 2010 as it was in 2000. The company also found itself up against a new style of competitor - social media savvy, content driven, fast moving companies that use the social Web to their advantage. To stay current, Eloqua needed to attract the attention of a new breed of influencer: marketing 2.0 and social media thought-leaders who'd amassed a following any magazine would respect.

The company was followed closely by marketing automation, e-mail and customer relationship management (CRM) insiders who knew it from years of direct experience, and it placed well in Gartner's Magic Quadrants and the Forrester Wave reports. But the broader universe of marketing influencers eluded the company.

Eloqua's goals were threefold: (1) make Eloqua more relevant in Web 2.0 and social media conversations, (2) attract a new breed of marketer to its website to discover marketing automation and (3) increase traffic to its new corporate blog.

Insight

With this in mind, Eloqua aimed to produce content that was so intrinsically valuable that influencers would have to pay attention. It applied the "earned media" concept to the social Web. It engaged in an "earned influence" program, and kicked off with a "steal our content" campaign in which it took high value internal resources and released them to the world. For free.

Creative Solution

Eloqua decided to make some of its internal resources public after a social media training session run by its Director of Content Joe Chernov. Joe Payne, CEO of Eloqua, sat in on the session and saw staff riffling through the physical Social Media Playbook - the incentive given out to reward those who attended the training - and asked, "What would happen if we made this book public?"

The question led to the marketing team taking inventory of what content was most likely to spread across the social Web. Ultimately, the team came full circle back to the resources Payne endorsed: The Content Grid and Social Media Playbook. Eloqua knew the benefits of being part of the Marketing 2.0 conversation would outweigh the risks of giving away "trade secrets" and the costs of hiring the industry's top design firm.

Content for the Taking

To ensure they earned the attention of influencers, Eloqua collaborated with A-list social media design firm JESS3 to fuse its compelling content with compelling design. In fact, the company's philosophy was "content = design;' reinforcing the notion that how something looks contributes directly to the public's perceived value of it.

The Content Grid is a visual depiction of content marketing that plots content type and distribution channel across two dimensions: who should create it (a single owner or the entire staff) and how it should be distributed for maximum impact on the sales funnel. The Content Grid was Eloqua's answer to the social Web's demand for visually striking infographics and desire for insight into the new "content marketing" phenomenon.

The playbook was a veritable how-to encompassing everything a person needed to know about social media. From Twitter to LinkedIn to Foursquare, any company (or individual) could take the playbook and run with it instantly.

To maximize impact, Eloqua released the documents back-to-back. First was The Content Grid, a visually captivating framework for content marketing. Then, just as the "buzz" for the info graphic began to dip, Eloqua published the Social Media Playbook, a veritable "how-to" guide on marketing via social networks. The market took notice immediately and now, months later, influencers continue to blog and tweet about the content.

The company also involved several influencers in the planning/design stage of the content so that when it was finally released, there would be a base level of support built in.

Gained Momentum

Eloqua sought to target three audiences: (1) the social media influencers who had eluded them in the past, (2) its core group of B2B marketing "insiders" and (3) people who tweeted/blogged about its competition, but not Eloqua. Eloqua knew that highly influential personalities would trigger a disproportion-ate amount of awareness, so it created an internal list of those it dubbed "super-influencers" and paid particular attention to their needs and interests.

35,000 downloads of The Content Grid/Social Media Playbook

The campaign earned the attention of super-influencers like Scott Monty (Ford), Jeffrey Hayzlett (celebrity CMO), Jennifer Aaker (Stanford), David Armano (Edelman) and Jeremiah Owyang (Altimeter Group) - people who had never before paid attention to Eloqua or marketing automation. WOMMA itself posted about the Social Media Playbook, writing in the WOMMA Word: " ... At most companies, such a document would be in the highly confidential, top-secret safe in the CEO's office. Not at Eloqua. They just gave it away for free ... and it's pretty amazing."

- Scott Monty summarized the impact and importance of Eloqua's Social Media Playbook when he wrote, " ...if I had this available to me some four years ago when I started this site, I would have been much smarter much more quickly. [It's] filled with exactly the kind of material that will bring you and your employees up to speed on social media."

- "In my opinion the Eloqua grid is equal to Geoffrey Moore's model from 'Crossing the Chasm' in both brilliance and clarity." – *Brian Hansford, Zephyr47*

- "Truly understanding your audience means looking at The Content Grid." – *Ken Yeung, bub.blicio.us*

- "Forward it on, this deserves to be shared. Very interesting blog too. Kudos to the crew over at Eloqua." – *Paul Armstrong, PaulArmstrong. Info*

- "It's a great way to think about corporate content marketing." – *Peter Kim, BeingPeterKim*

- "Put this in your next presentation that details your smarts on content generation, and then ask for a raise." – *DarrylOhrt, BrandFlakesForBreakfast*

- "I think Eloqua's new The Content Grid is fabulous: it crams a complex story and a lot of information into an easy-to-understand infographic on a critical topic for B2B and solutions marketing." – *Rob Leavitt, CustomerThink*

Results

On top of the resounding endorsements, Eloqua was able to map specific quantitative results back to its initial objectives:

- 12,000 new visitors to Eloqua's blog (instantly qualifying the twomonth-old blog for the Proteus top B2B blogs list)

- 35,000 downloads/views of The Content Grid/Social Media Playbook

- 2,600 tweets

- 56 blog posts

- 11 posts/tweets by AdAge Power l50

- 43% increase in traffic referred to Eloqua.com from blog

- 21 % increase in demo views (the company's top leading indicator for purchase)

- 12% increase in page views on Eloqua.com

- 14% decrease in "bounces" from Eloqua.com

Lastly, since this campaign and the training that precipitated it, not only are more staffers active on social media, but more importantly, "Eloquans" are finding their voices across a variety of networks. In addition to an increase in Twitter activity, some staffers have discovered blogging (four new bloggers!), others are contributing their photography to the company's new Flickr page, others are adding their decks to SlideShare and others are uploading their videos to YouTube. The success of this campaign has inspired a wave of content creation throughout the organization.

Who Else Is Exploring Word of Mouth? Recognize Any Of These Names?

From "The Anatomy of Buzz" the listed companies include: Amazon. com, AOL, Amway, Apple Computer, Armani, AT&T, Avon, Barnes & Noble, Blair Witch Project, BMW, Budweiser, Car & Driver Magazine, Charles Schwab, Cisco Systems, CNN, Coca Cola, Compuserve, Crisco Oil, DaimlerChrysler, Dell Computer, EBay, Edison, FedEx, Ford Mustang, General Motors, Harper & Row, Hewlett Packard, Honda, Intel, Intuit, Kodak, Lotus, Macy's, McDonald's, MCI, Microsoft, Miller Brewing, Neiman Marcus, Nike, Nintendo, Palm Computing, Pepsi, Polaroid, Proctor & Gamble, Saks Fifth Avenue, Star Wars, Sun Microsystems, Taco Bell, 3COM, Twentieth Century Fox, Union Bank of California, Warner Brothers, Yahoo, Ziff Davis.

From "The Secrets of Word of Mouth Marketing": Adobe, AOL, Apple, Avon, Campbell Soup, Citigroup, Dell, Disney, Eudora, First USA, Google, Hotmail, McKinsey & Company, Microsoft, Napster,

Roche Laboratories, United States Postal Service, Verizon DSL, Wall Street Journal, Xerox Parco

From "The Tipping Point"; ABC News, Airwalk Company, Audi Automobile, CBS, Centers for Disease Control, Century Wilshire Hotel, Coca Cola, Columbia Record Club, Glaxo Wellcome, Gore-Tex, Hush Puppies Shoes, New York City, Prozac, R.J. Reynolds, Sesame Street, TV Guide, Winston Cigarettes.

From "Unleashing the Ideavirus"; Academy of Motion Picture Arts and Sciences, Amazon, com, American Airlines, American Express, American Greeting, Amway, AOL, Apple, Atkins Diet, Audi, Barnes & Noble, Budweiser, Burger King, Cisco, Clairol, Coke, eToys, FedEx, Google, Hallmark, Harry Potter, Herman Miller, Hotmail, Intel, Kodak, Lycos, Marlboro, Mary Kay Cosmetics, McDonalds, MCI, McKinsey, Microsoft, Napster, Nike, Palm, PC Magazine, Polaroid, Post-it-Notes, Priceline, Reebok, Rexall, Schick, Sports Illustrated, Starbucks, Star Wars, Martha Stewart, 3M, Time Warner, Tommy Hilfiger, Toyota, ToysRUs, Tupperware, Twentieth Century Fox, VW Beetle, Yahoo.

The companies in the foregoing lists were referenced in the four books published on the topic of word of mouth/viral marketing around 2001. I cannot verify that these are all case studies of viral marketing, only that they touched the concept in some manner deemed worthwhile by the various authors.

Hotmail, Yahoo!, eBay, Amazon, GeoCities, Broadcast.com, Google —all of them succeeded because an ideavirus was unleashed and spread.

To reach 10 million users it took radio 40 years, TV 15 years, Netscape 3 years, and both Hotmail and Napster less than a year. Hotmail and Napster got the hang of viral marketing.

Choose Your Approach

There are several approaches for launching amplified word of mouth marketing, and they vary substantially, so it seems worthwhile to study them separately. While there is some disagreement, I see word of mouth as an umbrella covering varying approaches, namely influencer relations, viral marketing, and accelerated contagion. Each of these three will be explored more fully in its own chapter. According to WOMMA, variations of influencer relations include buzz marketing, community marketing, grassroots marketing, evangelist marketing, product seeding, cause marketing, and experiential marketing. This list could certainly be expanded and edited. Variations on the public relations industry concept of influencer relations are very popular. Equally powerful, but in a slightly different vein, are two approaches to viral marketing which I have arbitrarily divided into the Ideavirus approach and the Shockvirus approach.

Influencer Relations

From my friend Patrick Rooney of Expand Communications come the following thoughts: "What is Influencer Relations? Influencer Relations is a program to help ensure clients benefit from the lasting value of their relationships with elite industry influencers. The buying decisions of your customers are influenced by a far broader base than media and industry analysts, although each is vital to the overall communications mix. Today, the purchasing process is influenced by a broad array of friends, colleagues and peers, pundits, academics, authors, researchers, and many others. What's more, each market has its own set of influencers, making it necessary to understand how to identify, and then to reach, these new influencers. Simply put, the mantle of thought leadership and influence has fragmented, resulting in the need to expand your communications."

Regis McKenna summed it up well in his 1982 brochure on Word of Mouth which states, "Regarding the 90-10 Rule – by now one might be saying, 'Okay, by talking to everyone in the world we can better communicate our message. That's not practical or possible, Right!' But the 90-10 rule states that 90 percent of the world is influenced by the other 10 percent.

There are probably no more than 20 or 30 people in any one industry who have a *major* impact on trends, standards, opinion and a company's image or character.

Certainly we know this is true in the media and financial community. While there may be dozens of magazines and mountains of analysis covering an industry, only several have real influence and impact.

This is true within companies as well. A relatively few people hold the key to power in any organization. This is not to say that these key influences are easy to reach. A memo may reach them easier, but credible word-of-mouth approach will be far more influential and effective."

This review comes from a small brochure that Regis handed me in 1982 titled simply, *Word of Mouth*. Apparently I recognized something of value as I saved it for twenty-four years and recently shared it with WOMMA.

Other Influencers in the World of Influencers

Another equally prominent voice on the topic of influencers is that of Paul M. Rand, formerly Partner, Global Chief Development, and

Innovation Officer at Ketchum and Director of the firm's Global Technology Practice, but currently CEO of Zocalo Group.

Paul has led or co-led the development of four industry-recognized services: ChannelEdge (a sales channel communications program); Influencer Relationship Management (an influencer identification and marketing program); Women 25-54 (a service line focused on marketing to women) and Ketchum Personalized Media (delivering services in blogs, podcasts, Search Engine Optimization, and mobile marketing).

As the founder and CEO of Corporate Technology Communications (CTC), Paul led CTC into becoming the Midwest's largest independent corporate and technology communications firm and among the most respected in the nation. Ketchum acquired CTC in June 2001.

Market Research is Critical Too

To launch an influencers program you must start by getting management's acceptance of the principles of the Ed Keller/Jon Berry book on influencer relations titled *The Influentials*. CEO of the Keller Fay Group, Ed is known as "one of the most recognized names in word of mouth" and was president of WOMMA. The Keller Fay Group is the only full-service market research firm focused exclusively on word of mouth marketing. In April 2006, Keller Fay launched TalkTrack™, the first comprehensive tracking study of America's word of mouth conversations covering both offline word of mouth (which accounts for 90% of all conversation) as well as online. Prior to founding Keller Fay, Ed was the CEO of RoperASW.

To quote from Ed's book jacket, "For decades, the researchers at RoperASW have been on a quest for marketing's Holy Grail: that elusive but supremely powerful channel known as *word of mouth*. What they've learned is that even more important than the *"word"*—*what* is said – is the *"mouth"* – *who* says it. They've identified, studied, and analyzed influence in America since the Standard Oil Company of New Jersey (now Exxon) hired Elmo Roper himself to develop a model for identifying opinion leaders, and in *The Influentials* they are ready to share their results."

Launching a WOMM Program

The best approach is to build WOMM into a Marcom Engine (see Chapter 1) from which evolves your sales and marketing Communications Support Plan. The Marcom Engine blends the disciplines of Business Process Reengineering (BPR) with Integrated Marketing Communications (IMC) as well as concepts from Geoffrey Moore's TALC (technology adoption life cycle) approach in *Crossing the Chasm.* It drives revenue enhancement by fine-tuning the value proposition into the most compelling reason to buy, and by reducing the waste and inefficiency of the typical Random Task approach to marketing. Plus, it is the single most efficient way to manage a product launch.

Start by creating small buzzes first. The big one follows. An idiosyncrasy of word of mouth marketing is that before creating one contagious movement you have to create many small movements first. In other words, before you can fan the flames you have to ignite the fire.

A great book on the topic of fanning the flames is Greg Stielstra's exceptionally well-done *Pyro Marketing*, which I heartily endorse. To quote briefly, "The societal influences that allowed mass marketing to prosper have disappeared, rendering mass marketing ineffective. New circumstances have created an opportunity for a different marketing approach, called PyroMarketing. It involves four steps. 1. Promote to the people most likely to buy. 2. Give them an experience with your product or service. 3. Help them tell others. 4. Keep a record of who they are." The discussion continues to detail the creation of a successful marketing campaign, comparing the four steps above to the process of kindling a fire: "...*gather the driest tinder, touch it with a match, fan the flames, and save the coals.*" This is the essence of simplicity, and if you follow it religiously you will succeed.

Igniting the fire means that first you must understand the "Law of the Few" as defined by Malcolm Gladwell in his book *The Tipping Point.* He defines the "few" as Connectors, Mavens, and Salesmen. Spreading the word depends on people who are either experts or possessed of a rare set of social gifts. They're also called power influencers and evangelists. Found as spokes in your networks, they are further refined as regular hubs (non-media people), and mega hubs (media people).

Understanding Network Hubs

The following section on network hubs was extracted from Emanuel Rosen's *The Anatomy of Buzz* and Malcolm Gladwell's *The Tipping Point*, and then edited by Keith Bates.

> **NETWORK HUBS:** Network hubs are individuals who communicate with more people about a certain product than the average person does. Researchers have traditionally referred to them as "opinion leaders." In industry they're called "influencers," "lead users," or sometimes "power users."

There are two major types of "network hubs." Regular hubs are regular folks who serve as sources of information and influence in a certain product category and may be connected to only a few other individuals, or to several dozen. Mega-hubs comprise the press, celebrities, analysts, and politicians. According to Gladwell both these categories have subsets, known as Mavens, Connectors, and Salesmen.

Mavens (those who accumulate knowledge) are listened to because they have demonstrated significant knowledge of a certain area (at the very least, they have convinced others of their authority on a subject). Mavens tend to specialize in one narrow field of interest (movies, computers, corporate governance, litigation). To quote Gladwell, "Mavens are data banks."

Connectors are those people in every group who are more central because they are charismatic, are trusted by their peers, or are simply more socially active. Connectors know lots of the right kind of people. They act as social glue.

Again, to quote Gladwell, "Salesmen—with the skills to persuade us when we are unconvinced of what we are hearing...are as critical to the tipping of word-of-mouth epidemics as the other two groups."

Let me offer an easy acronym you can use to remember them: network hubs are ACTIVE. They are Ahead in adoption, Connected, Travelers, Information-hungry, Vocal, and Exposed to the media more than others. Network hubs are usually not the first to adopt a new product, but they are at least slightly ahead of the rest in their networks.

The fact is, not much is definitively known about network hubs; moreover, the nature of network hubs may differ from industry to industry. You won't find their names and addresses in any directory—identifying network hubs is substantially more complex than renting a mailing list. But the rewards for paying attention to these people can be huge.

Where Does One Find Network Hubs?

There are four methods commonly used:

1.Letting network hubs identify themselves. This means capturing the names of those who visit your website, or ask questions via email/snail mail.

2.Identifying *categories* of network hubs. Responses from ads in trade publications, or attendance at conferences, trade shows. However, these efforts primarily gather titles only.

3.Spotting network hubs in the field. To do this you must join a community, or solicit help from those already inside the community.

4.Identifying network hubs through surveys. Studies can be done online using such resources as RoperASW, Greenfield Online, or Opinion Research. Surveys can be subdivided into socio-metric, informant ratings, or self designating.

How to Work With Network Hubs

Tactics for interfacing with mega-hubs—"the media"—are well known by publicity people, and I have little new to offer here. What others do not usually discuss is how to go about reaching the millions of *regular hubs* who can spread news about a product. So I will focus here on reaching regular hubs.

The first tactical challenge in working with regular hubs is how to keep track of them. Building a system to record information about hubs is mostly a matter of making everyone at your organization aware of them. The database you build should have telephone numbers, e-mail addresses, and regular mailing addresses, as well as information about the scope and source of the hubs' influence and the nature of the networks *they belong to.*

Timing is important in communication with regular hubs, and seeding is often required. Here are a few tips to consider when spreading a message to your network of regular hubs:

- Target hubs first (before PR and ads)
- Give them something to talk about
- Stimulate them to teach others
- Give them the facts
- Don't abuse the relationships
- Be sure people see hubs using your product

Traps to watch out for:

The first trap to beware of is fixation on mega-hubs. If you focus on mega-hubs you leap to the dangerous conclusion that direct communication with customers is not important.

A second pitfall is too narrow an interpretation of network hubs. Don't focus on small elite group of influencers, go after 10% of the market. By the 90-10 rule (90% of your market is influenced by 10%), this is the right fraction to spread your message efficiently.

Thoughts on WOMM from Practitioners and Authors Plus Friends of the Author at both WOMMA (Word Of Mouth Marketing Assn.) and VBMA (Viral+Buzz Marketing Assn.)

Andy Sernovitz, the guy who, with some friends, founded the Word of Mouth Marketing Association in Chicago, recently published a book. In fact as I write this it is still hot off the press, because across the front cover of my copy is printed, "Advance review copy—not for sale." Following are a few quotes I can't resist copying.

"One of the most important things I've learned is that word of mouth marketing can be so easy and obvious that everyone misses just how easy and obvious it is. I get dozens of calls and emails every day from people asking how to get started. Small companies, big companies, everyone. There are a number of great books on the topic, but they are often high level or theoretical. It seems there isn't a simple how-to-get-started-with-word-of-mouth book."

"So, what is word of mouth marketing? In this book, I define it as "Giving people a reason to talk about your stuff, and making it easier for that conversation to take place." In the end, marketing is pretty easy: If people like your stuff, and if they trust you, they will tell their friends to do business with you. Learn to make customers really, really happy. It doesn't take much more than that. Understand this concept, devote yourself to it, and you will be a successful word of mouth marketer."

"This is nominally a book about a specific marketing technique. But it's really a new philosophy of business (and how to live it). It's about honesty and admiration. It's about making people happy. It's a simple philosophy, a new golden rule: Earn the respect and recommendation of your customers, and they will do the rest. Treat people well; they will do your marketing for you, for free.

Be interesting, or be invisible."

"One of the great misconceptions about word of mouth marketing is that it's all happening online. The role of the internet and the new ways people use it to communicate are indisputably critical components of the sudden spread of word of mouth. Blogs are a big deal because they empower lots of people to share ideas."

"For the first time in the history of modern business, we have a *force for good* that is also driven by the *all-powerful profit motive*. For years, government regulators and consumer advocates have tried to use legal and public pressure to make companies treat people well. I'll bet that the profit motive works better."

Andy makes another point that is worth thinking about regarding BtoB vs. BtoC. Although WOMM can be regarded as either one, in a certain sense it is something else entirely. It's not business to business, or business to consumer – it's consumer to consumer! Following is the word of mouth marketing manifesto from Andy's book. Read and heed.

The Word of Mouth Marketing Manifesto

1. Happy customers are your best advertising. Make people happy.

2. Marketing is easy. Earn the respect and recommendation of your customers. They will do your marketing for you, for free.

3. Ethics and good service come first.

4. UR the UE: You are the user experience (not what your ads say you are).

5. Negative word of mouth is an opportunity. Listen and learn.

6. People are already talking. Your only option is to join the conversation.

7. Be interesting, or be invisible.

8. If it's not worth talking about, it's not worth doing.

9. Make the story of your company a good one.

10. It is more fun to work at a company that people want to talk about. .

11. Use the power of word of mouth to make business treat people better.

12. Honest marketing makes more money.

George Silverman, *Secrets of Word-of-Mouth Marketing:* Word of mouth among business people and professionals (such as physicians, pharmacists, architects, and financial advisors) is very different from word of mouth for relatively low-ticket consumer products. The more expensive and complicated a product is, the more word of mouth comes into play. This is true because these products are more risky in terms of time, money, and potential damage to professional reputation. High-ticket products are not as easily tried as simple consumer products. People have to rely on other people's experience to substitute for all or part of the experience they would get in a trial.

Emanuel Rosen, *The Anatomy of Buzz:* My own experience with buzz has been mostly in the software industry ...

For buzz to spread, you need two things: a contagious product–one that has some inherent value that makes people talk—and someone behind the scenes who accelerates natural contagion. Yes, there are cases where having a great product or service alone is enough, but these typically occur when capacity is limited.

Technology markets, for example, are almost like presidential election campaigns, where there's no prize for second place. Winner takes all. In these markets the natural spread of word of mouth must be accelerated. Having a good product is not enough.

Don't be concerned about *boring* expert hubs. Dell Computer Corporation came to realize that network hubs are willing to spend twenty minutes with an ad and go through the specs and the features. That's why Dell's ads look like catalogs.

What kinds of products lend themselves to buzz? Products that somehow create high involvement among customers: Innovative products—like Netscape, and complex products—like software.

The more connected your customers are to each other, the more you depend on their buzz for future business. To see the full impact of this, look at a company like Cisco that has always served a tightly connected customer base. Cisco sells the hardware devices that glue the Internet together; almost by definition, all of its customers (network administrators and information technology managers) are heavy users of the Internet. "Our company started by word of mouth. There was no advertising," says Keith Fox, vice president of corporate marketing at Cisco. Since 1984, buzz about Cisco has been spreading relentlessly on the Net. Several Internet newsgroups are dedicated to Cisco's products.

Gabriel Weimann traces the notion of WOM all the way back to the Bible. When Moses complained to God that he could no longer control the people of Israel, God told him to gather "seventy men of the elders of Israel" and use them to spread the word to the rest of the people.

If you subscribe to the belief that we're all connected by a chain of no more than six mutual acquaintances then you might want to consider Emanuel's math: "Even in a small network that consists of only 100 people, there are 4,950 possible links among them. In a network with just 1,000 members there are almost *half a million* possible links!"

The spread of buzz, since it is not always easy to trace, tends to be neglected. To learn how to help create buzz, you should be able to answer these questions:

- From whom do your clients or customers typically learn about your product?

- What do people say when they recommend your product?

- How fast does information about your product spread compared with other products?

- Who are the network hubs?

- Where does the information hit a roadblock?

- How many sources of information does a customer rely on? Which ones are more important?

- What other kinds of information spread through the same networks?

It's crucial to understand that buzz about a product never spreads as simply as the two-step flow model would indicate—from company to media and mega-hubs, and from these hubs to the public. Yet the two-step model has been blithely assumed by countless companies over the years. There are two traps companies can fall into. The first is thinking that creating buzz is all about network hubs. If you exclusively focus on the two-step flow model, you can leap to the dangerous conclusion that direct communications with your customers is not important.

The second potential trap lies in a narrow interpretation of the term "network hubs." Almost all companies try to go after network hubs. But there's a big difference between going after an elite group of forty influencers and going after a broad, less visible population of four thousand of them. Numbers make a big difference in getting the word out. Many experts agree that the percentage of opinion leaders on average in the population is about 10 to 15 percent. But in practice, marketers sometimes target just a handful of "influencers"—not the full 10%.

The best buzz comes not from clever PR or advertising but rather from attributes inherent to the product itself. Contagious products can be grouped into six categories, as follows:

1. Products that evoke an emotional response. For most products and services it is usually the feeling of excitement and delight you get when your expectations are exceeded.

2. Products that advertise themselves. This type of product creates visual buzz by generating excitement simply by people viewing them in action.

3. Products that leave traces. These are products that self-propagate by leaving traces of themselves behind—paper trails or other evidence of their passing.

4. Products that become more useful as more people use them. Telephone, fax, and email are examples.

5. Products that are compatible. Products that fit peoples preexisting beliefs spread faster.

6. Products that "do the rest." Products that are easy to use spread faster because customers are hungry for simplicity. Example: Kodak's first camera copy line, "You press the button, we do the rest." When a customer has to explain just one step, her likelihood of completing the 'sales pitch' successfully is much higher than if she had to describe seven steps.

Always Exceed Expectations!

Cisco Systems serves network administrators who virtually live online, so you'd expect Cisco to use online methods to spread the word about its products. They do. But Cisco doesn't limit itself to the online world. The company organizes more than one thousand seminars every year to meet potential customers face to face, they organize networking events for their current customers, and they attend dozens of trade shows. Relationships with many customers start via face-to-face communication. The internet is used to maintain those relationships.

Does Madison Avenue Still Matter?

The truth is that very few products can rely on buzz alone. When used correctly, advertising can help buzz. However, it's also worth noting that ads can sometimes hurt genuine word of mouth. So in this section I want to focus on answering three questions:

1. Can advertising stimulate buzz? Absolutely. A good ad can help get people talking. (The shockvirus approach). It does so by jump-starting the process, reaching hubs, reassuring buyers, and getting the facts straight.

2. Can advertising *simulate* buzz? What about ads that masquerade as word of mouth? This is a tricky topic. You have to understand that an ad can hardly ever enjoy the credibility of buzz. Consider the "friendly" tone, testimonial advertising.

3. Can advertising kill buzz? Although there are many good reasons to advertise, advertising is a tool that should be used very cautiously if you want to promote buzz. Because advertising can also kill buzz when people feel that someone is shoving the message down their throats.

The six rules about ads and buzz:

1. Keep it simple. Messages need to be simple to be easily passed along.

2. Tell us what's new. Fluff doesn't travel well. Keep it relevant and newsworthy.

3. Don't make claims you can't support. Don't tell customers you care without proving it.

4. Ask your customers to articulate what's special about your product or service. Just ask!

5. Start measuring buzz. Very few ad agencies pretest for conversational impact. Helpful to ask two questions: Will the ad help network hubs answer questions they may get from other people in the networks? Will the ad stimulate members of the network to seek information from network hubs?

6. Listen to buzz. Monitor the network. Improve messaging.

The extensive buzz about high tech products is also driven by their complexity, which makes them difficult to evaluate. Talking with current users of a certain software package helps customers reduce the risk associated with the purchase.

Seth Godin, *Unleashing the Ideavirus:* Why do some viruses burn out more quickly than others? The simplest reason is that marketers get greedy and forget that a short-term virus is not the end of the process, it's the beginning. By nurturing the attention you receive, you can build a self-reinforcing virus that lasts and lasts and benefits all involved. Admit that few viruses last forever. Embrace the lifestyle of the virus.

5 Influencer Relations

Y ou should know that while I have chosen "influencer relations" as my focus for this book, WOMMA suggests that
other concepts/terms are synonymous, so I will share them
here with you. Influencer relations by other names may be
called buzz marketing, community marketing, grassroots marketing, evangelist marketing, product seeding, cause marketing, and experiential marketing. Messages may be distributed
in many ways, including through social media.

You should also know that influencer relations, while very potent,
are slow and reach relatively few people (but the right people).
Sustaining the needed network hubs can be very labor-intensive.
But it's worth it, as influencer relations are the source of quality
leads and shortened selling cycles.

OK, so you buy the concept of influencer relations. But where does
one begin? A fair question, and one that was posed to me recently in
the form of a comment which was in essence, "What's the big deal
about word of mouth? It's just another word for networking which
the company has been doing for years."

Networking vs. Influencer Relations

Are networking and influencer relations the same? Granted, there's a similarity, but that's all. In actual practice they are worlds apart. The difference could be compared to approaching a prospect through a well-guarded front door versus a vulnerable back door.

Another good simile is the situation that prompted my friend Melissa Giovagnoli to write her very popular book, featured on Oprah, called *Networlding*. In contrast to networking, the premise of *Networlding* proposes that instead of going to business functions and handing out business cards to strangers, you gather a circle of colleagues and develop those relationships. Ultimately they are much more rewarding...as long as you don't ignore the caveat of quid pro quo. Traditionally, people who do you a favor–like promoting your company – would like some favor done for them in return. Of course, you should be genuine in your relationships – we're talking about favors and not bribes – but if you develop your relationships with a view toward long-term symbiosis, you will reap great benefits.

The analogy between the concept of Networlding and influencer relations lies in the former being used as a process for building relationships that expand your career, while the latter works similarly to expand your business.

In the case of word of mouth influencers, rather than simply making cold calls to prospects you have identified, you develop relationships with people who are able to influence those prospects, and then help them to do so. Don't take my reference to cold calls too literally. Not many people do that anymore. But cold calls really represent that broad category of sales/marketing referred to by Seth Godin in his book Permissions Marketing as "interruption marketing." This is the opposite of "permission marketing" where you've been invited in. Influencer relations are not easy. They're complex, and they're time consuming...but they're incredibly potent at generating quality leads, and typically much less expensive than the old media blitz.

The major issue is simply one of credibility. People don't trust strangers. But they do trust friends and associates with whom they're familiar. WOMM gets you out of stranger mode. One-on-one with trusted acquaintances is the most effective way of changing the attitudes and beliefs that lead to changes in behavior.

Starting the Influencer Relations Process

The process of influencer relations starts by identifying segments of the business world that touch your prospects' business lives. Some samples of these segments include media, analysts, industry gurus, elite media, business leaders, associations, civic leaders, researchers, consultants, partners, academics, bloggers, government, legislature, groups, organizations, pundits, detractors, customer and vendor evangelists, etc. After marking out appropriate segments you must identity, contact, and nurture specific individuals within these segments who are receptive to your story.

What are some of the tactics employed in influencer relations? Paul Rand, formerly with Ketchum and the originator of IRM (Influencer Relations Management) allowed me to share some of his ideas in a recent PowerPoint presentation to the ITA (Illinois Technology Association).

To initiate a relationship you can employ face-to-face meetings, email or phone correspondence, direct response techniques regarding influencer work, product trials, information packages, forwarded articles of interest, and interaction at events. Opportunities for contact include recognitions awards, company conferences, spotlighting of influencers, briefings, webinars, road shows, and lunches or dinners.

To go to the next step, which is involvement, you might consider brainstorming among influencers, participation in a product review board or speakers bureau, testimonials, spending a day at the company, or a CEO summit meeting.

Compliments of Ketchum's IRM

The following outline is presented to you courtesy of Ketchum's recently introduced, proprietary IRM (Influencer Relationship Management) program. It uses a highly targeted approach rather than traditional mass media to identify, target, and connect with individuals and groups that can directly affect buyer's perceptions and behaviors. Their seven-step process follows:

1. Start the process of market segmentation and identification of the "Key Three" most critical proponents: initial influencers, ultimate influencers, and buyers and decision-makers.

2. Ecosystem and mapping is based on clearly determining desired mindset, actions, and impact of Key Three.

3. Prioritization and Benchmarking.

4. Strategic Alignment (program development).

5. Engagement.

6. Measure: With priorities, benchmarks, and programs, formalized IRM measures specific agreed-upon values.

7. Manage.

I like Paul's closing comment on Ketchum's website regarding IRM. "Influencing the influencers is not a new concept in the public relations world. Nearly every organization acknowledges the value and appreciates the impact of marketing influencers. Most companies, however, don't have a formal program in place to develop and manage these critical relationships. This is where Ketchum's IRM comes in."

From Regis McKenna on Influencer Relations

I made reference earlier to a small booklet given to me by Regis McKenna sometime between 1982 and 1984, and I'd like to share his thoughts on understanding the word of mouth structure particularly in reference to influencer relations:

"Word of mouth is so obvious a communications medium that we do not take the time to analyze or understand its structure. It is used, therefore, with much less direction and effectiveness than it could be used.

No marketing plan or communication plan contains a section called 'word of mouth:' it is implicit in the customer visits, sales training, public relations, and other elements of marketing. Peter Drucker once commented that more business decisions occur over lunch than at any other time of the day, yet no MBA courses are given on the subject.

The first task in defining the word-of-mouth network is to analyze and understand its nature. Networks exist in each of these areas:

- From one management level to another, and from one worker to another. Moving information through the organization for assimilation and direction cannot be by 'thunderbolt.' Effective communication is better absorbed and used by person-to-person communication. One-on-one and small group meetings avoid the problems of misinterpretation.

While memoranda may contain all the correct information, they do not carry the interface mechanisms to gain commitment, support, and understanding.

- The financial community network chain. It is often said that it is far more important who backs a company than how much money is behind it. Obtaining the 'correct' initial investors depends on what is 'said' about you and your idea.

The venture capital and private investor network is a relatively small, close- knit community. Within it, word spreads rapidly about a good idea.

As the company moves to go public, the word of mouth spreads from the original investors to the investment bankers, commercial bankers, analysts, and brokers more by telephone than any other means.

- The customer word-of-mouth chain. Although this chain varies from industry segment to industry segment, each one has a network forum for word of mouth, including industry conferences, trade shows, technical conferences, seminars, sales calls, training and education programs, 'seeding' a champion within the customer organization, and phone calls. In launching a new product in the equipment and systems business, the beta sites become all-important. The first users become the all-important credible reference and base for a word-of-mouth program.

- The industry watchers and other third parties. Recently, the industry watchers, market analysts, and industry experts have become more important in the electronics industry. As the industry becomes more and diversified, there has become more of a need for interpreters, soothsayers and futurists.

Practically every article on any aspect of the electronics business requires comment by one or two of the industry watchers to provide credibility. Yet these industry watchers obtain their information by visiting companies, attending analysts' meetings, talking to people in the industry and so forth. It is often joked that forecast numbers make a full cycle.

- **The press and its sources.** Over 90 percent of the major news stories written in the business and technical press come from direct conversations. When a journalist is on to a story, he or she begins searching the network for background, opinions, verification, and challenges. Each journalist has a network that constantly changes and grows with each story. If one's views are not verified by the network or are challenged by the network, the story will take on a different character.

- **The selling chain.** The information in any one company moves from product marketing and sales management out to regional sales or representative organizations. Then the information is relayed through distributors and application engineers to the customer.

These people may know what to sell, how much it costs, and even when to sell, but the enthusiasm, the rallying behind the commitment, the picture of the future, and the character of the management and the company all come through word of mouth.

- **The community.** Every person who is interviewed or delivers a package or visits one's company walks away with an impression. Certainly, the physical environment is important, but the interpersonal experiences will be the most critical verified communication to the community. If it is done properly, every employee prospect, whether he or she is hired or not, becomes a salesperson for the company. Every visitor and vendor becomes a 'carrier' for the company's word."

6 Viral Marketing

> "It took radio 40 years to reach 10 million users, TV only 15 years, Netscape 3 years, and both Hotmail and Napster less than a year. Hotmail and Napster got the hang of viral marketing. Have you?"

The Origin of Viral Marketing

Viral marketing is the management of an "ideavirus" or a "shockvirus" through word of mouth online. It's word of mouth on steroids. Some of those steroids are social media, Facebook in particular.

It's marketing's response to the educated consumer and the Internet. As the ability (speed) of customers to communicate with customers grows stronger, the credibility of marketers communicating with customers grows weaker. If charging people for exposure to your virus is going to slow down its spread, give it away! Apple cut the price of WebObjects from \$50,000 to \$699, recognizing that unless *a lot of people* used their software, no one would use it!

What's this viral marketing thing all about? Viral marketing (VM) is defined as *managing* digitally-augmented word of mouth, or buzz. "Digitally-augmented" simply means using the internet to deploy your VM program, with email as the primary tool of choice. Word of mouth has been around since the beginning of time, but without electronic support its spread was both tedious and slow from a marketing standpoint. The internet has changed all that.

A Five Step Process for Getting the Word Out

1. Why do you believe your idea is virusworthy?

First define your hive, or desired viral environment (small enough that you can dominate). Then, for the answer to this question ask yourself "why" five times, each time delving deeper into your answer.[1]

After each answer ask "why" of that answer. No flip responses. If it's not worth talking about, it won't get talked about. You must have a USP (Unique Selling Proposition), and it should be a consensus of sales, marketing, management, and engineering input. Also it must fill a vacuum.

[1] The 5 Whys process was developed by Taaichi Ohno for Toyota over 30 years ago. Today it's an important part of the famous Six Sigma approach to improving operational performance. The 5 Whys is a unique problem solving technique.

2. What is the message you wish to distribute?

Gather message input from all levels of your consumer base by polling users, pundits, power influencers. Use qualitative research (online/face-to-face focus groups). The best message would be a consistent 5-word phrase. Variables to consider in building your virus are nature of the sneezers, makeup of the hive, importance of digital augmentation, vector (where it starts, best resonates, path of least resistance), medium/vehicle for distribution, ease of sharing, persistence/the stickiness factor, and amplification through interruption advertising (accelerated contagion). And remember, people are more apt to spread the word about specifics than simply to spread general praise. Stay focused.

3. Who are the people best qualified to start your viral epidemic?

Define the *environment* (referred to as a hive in viralspeak), and the *distributors,* known either as *sneezers,* (both powerful and promiscuous), or *network hubs,* (both regular and mega, and made up of mavens, connectors, persuaders – see Chapter 4). In order to achieve a viral campaign, 100 sneezers seems to be the magic number. It's important that *you choose* them. Develop evangelists among customers, employees, suppliers, and the press. *Power* sneezers can't be bought, but can be selfishly motivated. One challenge is locating the regular network hubs who will spread your message (discussed in Chapter 4). Brace yourself...the better the product, the more difficult its acceptance (chasm to Main Street).

4. Which communications vehicles work best to get the word out?

Customer/employee referrals, support materials, events for customers who desire to disseminate the word, seeding the market, canned distribution (audio, video, web, collateral), user groups, web communities, discussion groups (teleconferences, webinars, seminars, regional conferences), loyalty programs, industry focused advisory groups, electronic coupons, email, direct mail, broadcast fax, stories to spread, newsletters, article series, blogging, high profile product placement, speaking engagements, customer/employee evangelism training, Networlding, sampling, writing a book, and influencing rating services. Also critical is an understanding of decision acceleration. Don't overlook "virals," which are basically shallow but memorable viruses – think of them as the equivalent of a 20-second TV spot that demands sharing.

5. When will the viral marketing launch begin?

Launch begins after virus-worthiness is established, the message is cast in stone, and all traditional sales pitches, marcom materials, and press releases have been fine-tuned for consistency. Typically 30 to 60 days from startup depending on management zeal. Parting thought—rather than the *decreasing returns* delivered by traditional advertising (interruption marketing), an ideavirus offers *increasing returns* because the more people have the product, the more people want it. For inspiration, read Silverman's "Twenty-Eight Secrets of Word-of-Mouth Marketing." (included in Chapter 8).

Ideavirus vs. Shockvirus: Which to Use

An Ideavirus is about the *concept of the product* while a Shockvirus is about the *presentation of the product.* One is about good ideas and the other about good presentations. Traditionally great ideas last longer than great presentations. Although the lines are blurring today, you may be exposed to either ideaviruses or shockviruses, depending on where you live. Viral marketing in the UK is a little different than the early efforts of viral marketing in the US. Their leading practitioners seem to depend more on powerful graphics than unique product attributes to convey the power of the product. They focus more on "shockviruses" than "ideaviruses" – simply a different school of thought. Both are effective.

The Ideavirus was really the pioneering viral marketing catalyst and traces the concept of its origin back to Geoffrey Moore's *Crossing the Chasm* where he discusses technology adoption, "...any time we are introduced to products that require us to change our current mode of behavior or to modify other products and services we rely on ... such change-sensitive products are called *discontinuous innovations*. The contrasting term, *continuous innovations*, refers to the normal upgrading of products that do not require us to change behavior."

Ideaviruses represent discontinuous product innovations. I like Geoffrey Nicholson's (VP Technical Planning/Technical Ops for 3M) statement from some years back that I saved. "If an idea doesn't stop people in their tracks, then maybe it's just an incremental change and not an innovation at all."

If your product is original enough, it will lend itself naturally to an Ideavirus campaign. However a less radical product can be highly successful with the right Shockvirus marketing. You must think long and hard about which approach is best.

Launching an Ideavirus

To quote Seth Godin again from *Unleashing The Ideavirus*, "...to embrace ideavirus marketing techniques you also have to accept a change from the status quo. And many of the executives who are now in charge made their way to the top by embracing the status quo, not fighting it." Convincing these executives to reach out to 100 influencers in order to start a viral campaign may take some doing.

The challenge I've encountered is with startup companies who don't have a hundred users and are reluctant to give product away, or with established companies who get a lot of money for their product and are reluctant to give up any income. These giveaways should be considered beta sites...or investments in sales and marketing.

Exploring the Shockvirus, Another Viral Approach

Shockviruses are typified by shocking graphics and tend to rely more on entertainment and visual excitement for their virus-worthiness than product differentiation. UK creative giants Digital Media Communications Ltd. (DMC) and The Viral Factory were early proponents of this approach. Ideaviruses traditionally have relied more on unique product attributes, although that is changing rapidly as I write this.

Shockviruses tend to have a shorter life than ideaviruses because ideaviruses are dependent on powerful, discontinuous product innovations, while any brilliant creative director can come up with a shockvirus.

Because shockviruses will wear out their welcome once the newness and excitement grow old, you must explore ways to augment or reinforce your message. Augmentation typically uses traditional integrated direct marketing programs, whether ongoing or of the 90-Day Blitz variety, and is often supported by public relations. Viral augmentation tactics will also be heavily dependent on the Internet.

Launching a Shockvirus

The first challenge to getting started with the Shockvirus approach is locate a production firm with the creative expertise and experience to build a virus so provocative that it spreads to epidemic proportions...like the recent Subservient Chicken from Burger King.

The second challenge is then to assign a viral marketing / creative consultant to work with the production company who understands the product and market well enough to keep the viral creative on track. This person could come from the ranks of creative consultants or interactive ad agency creative.

What should you expect in the way of deliverables from your viral marketing resource, whether in-house or outsourced?

- Start with the development of a virusworthy product, to be achieved either through recommended product modifications or a new positioning strategy.

- Then define and develop databases of power influencers, both regular hubs and mega-hubs.

- Next is development of messages, assistance with seeding of the networks and multiple forums, event strategies, and virus maintenance recommendations based on context sensitivity.

- And finally comes development of the accelerated contagion process to sustain both the influencer relations and the viral campaign.

3 Easy Steps to Startup...

1. **Assemble a Viral Marketing team** consisting of internal sales and marketing people, a VM consultant who can also support ad needs, and a PR firm. Keep in mind that traditional

advertising and PR work well at supporting established brands, they just do a poor job of getting them established in the first place.

2. **Start the process** of identifying and developing Regular and Mega levels within your network hubsdatabases...and then move on to the more difficult steps of follow through:

3. **Develop virus-worthiness** concept/strategy

4. **Write copy** to support ideavirus/generate buzz

5. **Expose the virus** through regular/mega hubs.

6. **Use the 90-Day Blitz** to support epidemic.

7. **Maintain/reinforce virus** before apathy sets in.

7 Accelerated Contagion

> *"...smart marketers know that word of mouth almost always needs help. They do something to make that word spread faster."*
>
> *"Two things are needed to create buzz successfully. The first one is to have a contagious product. But having such a product alone is not enough. Companies that get good buzz also accelerate natural contagion."*
>
> *"Technology markets, for example, are almost like presidential election campaigns, where there's no prize for second place. Winner takes all. In these markets the natural spread of word of mouth must be accelerated. Having a good product is not enough."*
>
> Excerpts above from Emanuel Rosen's The Anatomy of Buzz.

Accelerated Contagion works equally well for word of mouth or traditional integrated direct marketing. Whether through influencer relations, viral marketing, or evangelism, it will make your approach to word of mouth marketing work better. Besides adding visibility and muscle to your sales and marketing, it speeds up the distribution of your word of mouth – regardless of your approach. Points to consider:

- Influencer relations, while potent, are slow and reach relatively few people. Sustaining influencer relations can be very labor-intensive.

- Viral marketing, while potent also, is fast, and if done well, it reaches many people. But virals are typically short-lived, so that accelerated contagion is critical to sustain the awareness generated by the viral.

- Cultivating evangelists can be tedious work in that it is often difficult to find volunteers who will take a leadership role, and the numbers reached are small.

So what do we do? Expand your numbers!

What accelerated contagion does is to expand the numbers for influencer relations, add longevity to your viral marketing, and raise public exposure for evangelism. What must be done after you build your WOMM program is simply to add an accelerated contagion component. Specifically:

- Accelerated contagion is a multimedia, lead-generation activity based on response compression techniques.

- It is a fully integrated 3-month program that combines traditional media with electronic media to create a sense of event, which in turn produces a substantial flow of leads in a very short time with minimal commitment of financial resources.

Accelerated contagion is a proven process with a long history of successes! The process evolved from the teachings of Ernan Roman in a document subtitled "The Cutting-Edge Strategy for Synchronizing Advertising, Direct Mail, Telemarketing and Field Sales." It was published in 1995 and for ten years proved itself with dozens of Bates' software vendor clients under the label, 'The 90-Day Blitz.' Since that time it has been adapted into accelerated contagion to serve WOM Marketing.

Accelerated contagion is a way of adding teeth to your word of mouth marketing management. It lets you be a tiger!

Accelerated contagion and response compression

To quote Ernan Roman, author of *Integrated Direct Marketing*, "We have found that the traditional sequencing of media does not create the maximum synergy from the media being employed. Specifically, the impressions are conveyed over too long a time period, diluting the impact to a significant degree ... we create a sequence of ongoing contacts, using a variety of media. These are deployed with short, carefully orchestrated intervals between contacts so that we gain a disproportionate share of the prospect's attention. A sense of event is generated - a feeling that something important is going on. It would be far more difficult, if not impossible to achieve this effect through isolated media. We call this tighter time-frame approach 'response compression'. By deploying media in an abbreviated time frame, we create an intensified synergy between media that generates much higher response rates."

Media for accelerated contagion runs the gamut from microsites, search engine optimization and marketing, blogs, forums, email, podcasting, voice and fax broadcasting, telemarketing, direct mail, tradeshows, webinars, print media, broadcast, experiential, promotion, seeding, CGM (consumer- generated media), and evangelism ... plus others.

Prior to the advent of the internet, integrating media was simpler and often consisted of only a letter or postcard, a full page trade publication ad, and a broadcast fax supported by telemarketing to a well-tested house list. Accelerated contagion is successful because of its adaptive incorporation of new and evolving digital media.

Accelerated Contagion
Goals and Objectives

Goals of accelerated contagion include sales acceleration and increased market awareness. The challenge is to do this quickly, and within a manageable budget. Specifically, accelerated contagion is designed to:

- expand the numbers of contacts for influencer relations
- add longevity to the impact of your viral marketing
- raise public exposure and product enthusiasm via evangelism.

Sales/marketing problems that prompt the contagion strategy often include poor response levels to present marketing communications efforts, a return on investment of marketing dollars that is poor or not measurable, and a high sales cost caused by ineffective media strategies. Other concerns may include long cycle times due to low market awareness or bad positioning, delay of marketing messages, and quarterly and/or annual sales goals not being met. Often the most serious core issue is failure to find a Lightning Bolt or Big Idea that reaches the "feeling" side of your prospects. You must sell the sizzle, not the steak (the classic selling of features, not benefits, by recognizing that people typically buy based on emotion and use logic to justify the purchase).

A major benefit of accelerated contagion is its ability to help technology vendors, focused on fast growth, in fusing the traditionally adversarial disciplines of sales and marketing into the single business process of sales/marketing communications. The Marcom Engine drives this process, but to gain a competitive edge you should know that the SECRET OF SUCCESS in employing accelerated contagion lies in skillful blending of the media!

How to Be a Relevant CMO: Word of Mouth and Accelerated Contagion

According to a Brand Autopsy Report of several years ago, factors driving the trend toward shrinking CMO tenures include misaligned performance expectations, over-promising and under-delivering, and a poor cultural fit.

What are the top CEO priorities? According to Booz Allen Hamilton they are top-line growth; speed, flexibility, and adaptability to change; customer loyalty and retention; and stimulating innovations.

From a study by the CMO Council – "tech marketers ranked lead generation as the most important way to measure marcom performance." What's your ROI for "qualified" lead generation activities?

If you are a CMO who needs marketing dexterity for your work to flourish – or perhaps for your career to survive – you should examine the power in Word of Mouth marketing, and then you should explore accelerated contagion. Following is the executive summary of the Booz Allen Hamilton report.

Booz Allen Hamilton Report
Are CMO's Irrelevant? Executive Summary

Marketers are in the jaws of a paradox. Although new communications technologies, fragmenting audiences, and rising customer demands for increasingly individualized products and services would seem to render their knowledge and skills more relevant than ever, senior marketing executives say they are receding farther from the centers of influence in their companies.

In collaboration with the Association of National Advertisers, the leading U.S. marketing trade organization, Booz Allen Hamilton surveyed 370 people at more than 100 companies in nine industries in an attempt to discover whether marketing is in fact disconnected from the leadership agenda, and if so to determine the causes of this dysfunction. An additional aim was to uncover the best practices of superior marketing organizations.

The study found three organizational dichotomies hindering the effectiveness of marketing organizations:

1. More than 75 percent of marketers and non-marketers say that marketing has become more important to their companies during the past five years. But at more than half of all companies, marketing and the CEO agenda are not aligned.

2. Higher expectations for marketing have driven nearly 70 percent of all companies to reorganize their marketing departments during the same period. But a major question in many such reorganizations – the position of chief marketing officer – remains unanswered.

3. Measurable outcomes are now expected for marketing programs–66 percent of executives say true ROI analytics are marketing's greatest need. But most companies are still

using surrogate metrics, such as awareness, instead of ROI measurements.

Among other recommendations, the ANA/Booz Allen study advises that companies clearly choose from among three emerging CMO models– Marketing Service Provider, Marketing Advisor, or Driver of Growth–to find a role appropriate to the individual company. The study also recommends companies develop an "expectations" contract between the CEO and the marketing organization that sets a clear organizational structure, establishes decision rights, promotes the development of capabilities such as ROI analytics and consumer insights, and encourages appropriate risk taking in pursuit of business, i.e. building ideas.

" Word of mouth marketing is...
"Giving people a reason to talk about
your stuff and making it easier for
that conversation to take place." "

Conclusion: Call to Action for WOMM

Now that we understand the concept behind word of mouth marketing and the various tools required for its implementation, perhaps it's time to consider putting it work for us.

Tell me again why I need WOMM.

It's not an overnight panacea for inadequate lead flow, but it offers a powerful resource for adding credibility to your marketing messages: something that is sorely needed in a world that just doesn't want to hear it anymore from traditional marketers. It's the secret weapon behind *qualified* leads.

Why the departure from tradition? Traditional marketing is just not effective anymore because the speed of information diffusion, enabled by the internet, is weakening the ability of *companies* to communicate with customers and strengthening the ability of *customers* to communicate with customers. An effective WOMM campaign will establish a foundation process whereby interested people market to each other.

Inspired by Metcalfe's law, case studies, and practitioners' comments, where do we begin? You begin by making an assessment of your product, your market, and your marketing needs. This leads to a choice about which is best – a corporate contact program to influencers, or a virals program employing customer word of mouth, or both – plus accelerated contagion to keep it alive.

Consider the market. How great is the need for your product? And how will your message be received, i.e. is your product/ service really innovative or just incrementally better? Finally, take into account your needs, which are influenced to a certain degree by the marketing dollars available. Would a low-key, slower-moving influencer program do the job? Or do you want to gamble on a fast-return viral effort? Many people do both, because there is a similarity in the startup procedure relative to the development of customer and influencer databases.

Creative is key when launching WOM! Messaging concepts, copy, and graphics will largely determine the success of your venture – assuming you have something the market needs, and can get excited about. But remember to integrate that messaging within an entire communications support plan, which must embrace and include the sales force (whether direct, channel, or OEM) as well.

Understand your network hubs. Without a good set of names, researched through both primary and secondary research, you have no place to begin. Because network hubs are so crucial, you may wish to reread [here, give a reference by chapter and section heading] before proceeding.

If you're ready to put WOM into action, revisit www.womma.org, not only for its wealth of information but for the listings of resources among its membership.

**Word of Mouth Marketing defined
by Andy Sernovitz, founder of WOMMA**

8 Word of Mouth Marketing as Described by Practitioners

The following pages contain summaries/edits I have written of six of the books listed below.* These summaries have been extracted from my monthly blog written a few years ago, and reflect the development of a fascinating field which grows stronger every day, particularly with the advent of social media. I am personally acquainted with most of the people listed below, many of whom have had a powerful influence in shaping my knowledge and opinions regarding word of mouth, influencer relations, and viral marketing over the past years. For that I am very grateful. They are listed in the order we met.

- Regis McKenna, *Word of Mouth*
- Malcolm Gladwell, *The Tipping Point**
- Seth Godin, *Unleashing the Ideavirus**
- Emanuel Rosen, *The Anatomy of Buzz**
- George Silverman, *Secrets of Word of Mouth Marketing**
- Jackie Huba/Ben McConnell, *Creating Customer Evangelists**
- Ed Keller and Jon Berry, *The Influentials**

Regis McKenna, *Word of Mouth*

The difference between word of mouth and *all* other forms of communication include:

- It is an experienced process, rather than an observed one. The message in word of mouth is embodied in a living, breathing, emotional person.

- The message is tuned to the individual listener. It is changed, simplified, altered, embellished and verified for each person.

- The credibility of the speaker carries over to the message immediately.

- Experts can be used in this medium without the negative effect of commercializing his or her position and message.

- Efficiency; while word of mouth takes time to disseminate, the message is delivered directly to those who must use the information and act on it.

- Feedback is instantaneous: agreement, disagreement, understanding, not understanding.

Malcolm Gladwell's *The Tipping Point*

In this brilliant and groundbreaking book, *New Yorker* writer Malcolm Gladwell looks at why major changes in our society so often happen suddenly and unexpectedly. Ideas, behavior, messages, and products, he argues, often spread like outbreaks of infectious disease. Just as a single sick person can start an epidemic of the flu, so too can a few fare-beaters and graffiti artists fuel a subway crime wave, or a satisfied customer fill the empty tables of a new restaurant. These are *social* epidemics, and the moment when they take off, when they reach their critical mass, is the Tipping Point.

Gladwell introduces us to the particular personality types who are natural pollinators of new ideas and trends, the people who create the phenomenon of word of mouth. He analyzes fashion trends, smoking, children's television, direct mail, and the early days of the American Revolution for clues about making ideas infectious, and visits a religious commune, a successful high-tech company, and one of the world's greatest salesmen to show how to start and sustain social epidemics.

What You'll Learn in *The Tipping Point*:

Directions for reaching a Tipping Point. You'll learn how the three rules of the Tipping Point – the Law of the Few, the Stickiness Factor, and the Power of Context – offer a way of making sense of epidemics.

How to choose the people who will spread the epidemic. You'll learn how to identify mavens, connectors, and salesmen (persuaders).

The importance of memorable product exposure. The Presentation is everything. If your product is not inherently exciting you must position your message so that it is, and has the ability to move people.

Understanding the power of context. You'll learn to become sensitive to the circumstances and conditions of times and places, those specific and relatively small elements in the environment that can serve as Tipping Points.

Seth Godin, *Unleashing the Ideavirus*

If you don't have time to read the whole book, here's what it says: Marketing by interrupting people isn't cost-effective anymore. You can't afford to seek out people and send them unwanted marketing messages in large groups and hope that some will send you money. Instead, the future belongs to marketers who establish a foundation and process where interested people can market to each other. Ignite consumer networks and then get out of the way and let them talk.

Why Ideas Matter. The holy grail for anyone who traffics in ideas is this: to unleash an ideavirus. An idea that just sits there is worthless. But an idea that moves and grows and infects everyone it touches ...that's an ideavirus. An ideavirus is a big idea that runs amok across the target audience. Word of mouth is not new, it's just different now. Ideaviruses give us increasing returns: word of mouth dies out, but ideaviruses get bigger. And finally, ideaviruses are the currency of the future. While ideaviruses aren't new, they're important because we're obsessed with the new, and an ideavirus is always about the new.

The key steps for Internet companies looking to build a virus are:

- Create a newsworthy online experience that's either totally new or makes the user's life much better. Or makes an offline experience better/faster/cheaper so that switching is worth the hassle.

- Have the idea behind your online experience go viral, bringing you a large chunk of the group you're targeting without having to spend a fortune advertising the new service.

- Fill the vacuum in the marketplace with your version of the idea, so that competitors now have a very difficult time of un-teaching your virus and starting their own.

- Achieve "lock in" by creating larger and larger costs to switching from your service to someone else's.

- Get permission from users to maintain an ongoing dialogue so you can turn the original attention into a beneficial experience for users and an ongoing profit stream for you.

- Continue creating noteworthy online experiences to further spread new viruses, starting with your core audience of raving fans.

Emanuel Rosen, *The Anatomy of Buzz*

Emanuel Rosen, with nine years experience as Marketing VP for a Silicon Valley software company, here illuminates the reality of how "buzz" can be launched and managed so as to more rapidly reach a critical mass (the tipping point) of adopters for one's innovation.

What You'll Learn in *The Anatomy of Buzz*

How buzz spreads. You'll learn that buzz is all the word of mouth about a brand, which it spreads through invisible networks of very special people, that we talk because we're programmed to talk, and that nothing happens without the establishment of network hubs. You'll also learn the structure of these networks and about the energy and credibility required to make it work.

How to assure success. You'll learn that some products evoke an emotional response, some advertise themselves, some leave traces, others become more useful as people use them. Some products are compatible, and others "do the rest." You'll discover the power of gossip. And you'll learn that there's still a need for traditional advertising, promotion, and PR to accelerate the whole process, but that the timing of this stuff is critical. It's called Leapfrogging, and it builds momentum.

How to stimulate the spread of buzz. You'll learn how to identify and nurture network hubs, the importance and techniques of "seeding," and the importance of having a good story. You'll learn to think of viral marketing as a buzz accelerator, and you'll realize that very few products can rely on buzz alone. You'll gain skills at channel deployment, but at the same time discover that ads can hurt as well as help. And lastly you'll read examples of people who did it and how, followed by a Buzz Workshop chapter that Seth Godin says "by itself is worth the entire price of the book!"

George Silverman, *The Secrets of Word of Mouth Marketing*

Twenty-Eight Secrets of Word-of-Mouth Marketing

#1. Selling is mostly an illusion.

#2. By influencing word of mouth directly, sales can be increased 3x to 10x.

#3. Single most effective method for speeding up decisions is word of mouth.

#4. Word of mouth is as easy to structure and use as traditional advertising.

#5. Word of mouth is literally thousands of times as powerful as advertising.

#6. Word of mouth is paradoxically the most powerful neglected force in mktg.

#7. It is almost impossible for your product to succeed unless it has massive positive word of mouth.

#8. Word of mouth either explodes at an exponential rate or it fizzles.

#9. There are over a dozen reasons why word of mouth is so powerful. All of these reasons, once understood, can be turned to your advantage.

#10. What gives WOM its power is that it's an experience delivery mechanism.

#11. There are many different types of WOM, all potentially controllable.

#12. Different types of decision makers need different types of word of mouth at each stage of the decision cycle.

#13. As important as content is, the sequence and source are just as important.

#14. There are basically two levels of word of mouth, expert and peer, and their relative power varies at different stages of the decision cycle.

#15. In word of mouth marketing, confirmation and verification are more important that information.

#16. In word of mouth marketing, you are navigating spheres of influence.

#17. Experts are more approachable that ordinary people, but only through total honesty.

#18. Credibility is more important in an expert than fame.

#19. There are many reliable mechanisms for delivering word of mouth.

#20. Word of mouth must be approach systematically, as a campaign.

#21. The word of mouth among your sales force can be more important than the word of mouth among your customers.

#22. There is a specific way to research the naturally occurring word of mouth so that you can identify exactly what your customers are actually saying.

#23. There is a way to experiment with ways to influence the natural word of mouth and verify that it is in fact persuasive.

#24. There are many ways of producing and delivering "canned" word of mouth that are almost as powerful as live, spontaneous word of mouth.

#25. Paradoxically, in word of mouth, unlike in conventional marketing, negatives can be more reassuring than positives about the product.

#26. "Word-of-mouth advertising is a contradiction in terms.

#27. In word of mouth marketing, any perceived attempt to influence the content will totally invalidate the communication.

#28. The usual rules of advertising and salesmanship are often counter-productive in word of mouth marketing.

Jackie Huba/Ben McConnell, *Creating Customer Evangelists*

You are an evangelist. You tell others what movie to see, which computer to purchase, what restaurant to visit, which dentist you prefer, which cell phone to buy, which books to read, which clubs to join. Your recommendations are sincere. Passionate, perhaps.

How to Spot Evangelists and What to Do with Them

People talk about you. They talk about your company, your products and services, and your personality. Many say nice things, and some are absolutely gushy with their praise. Would you like to know who they are? How do you find your evangelists? Here are a few ideas.

Scan the Web using your favorite search engine and discover where you are mentioned online and by whom. Make note of everyone who compliments your products and services and everyone who criticizes them. For the people who love you, send them a hand-written thank-you note. For those who take issue with your products or services, find a way to contact them via e-mail or ask if it's OK to talk on the phone.

Ask prospective customers specifically how they discovered you. If it was from a friend or colleague, ask the prospect for the name of the referrer. Keep detailed records of how people discovered you.

If you have an opt-in e-mail list, add a field that asks how people discovered you. Continually refine the quantifiable nature of this field. You want to gather as much information as possible from this field, especially if the referrals are from people. Those are your evangelists!

Be an active participant in e-mail discussion lists and online bulletin boards that your customers frequent. Watch for customers who post recommendations about you. Cultivate relationships with them. Keep them in your loop.

Use website tracking software to understand how website visitors discover you. If customers, prospects, fans, or evangelists link to your site, do *not* send them a cease-and-desist letter. This creates customer vigilantes, not customer evangelists.

Ed Keller and Jon Berry, *The Influentials*

One American in ten tells the other nine how to vote, where to eat, and what to buy. They are **The Influentials.**

Who are they? The most influential Americans– the ones who tell their neighbors what to buy, which politicians to support, and where to vacation–are not necessarily the people you'd expect. They're not America's most affluent 10 percent or best-educated 10 percent. They're not the "early adopters," always the first to try everything from Franco-Polynesian fusion cooking to digital cameras. They are, however, the 10 percent of Americans most engaged in their local communities...and they wield a huge amount of influence within those communities.

Six Rules for Getting into the Conversation

What's your influential strategy? If you've not asked yourself this question already, you should. To succeed today, you need to connect with the people who are at the center of the conversation. Business, government, and nonprofit organizations need to have influential strategies just as they need marketing, advertising, public relations, promotion, or internet strategies.

Specifically, you should make sure you are reaching the decision-makers who are influential in others' decisions. You should know where the opinion leaders get *their* ideas–the kinds of publications they read, the programs they watch, the radio stations they listen to, and the websites they go to. You should make sure you don't have the door shut when opinion leaders come to you with a complaint or question.

You should be out in the community to make sure you're listening to opinion leaders' concerns. You should pay attention to what's happening in opinion leaders' lives, the issues that opinion leaders are reading up on, the problems they are focused on, and their short- and long-term goals. Companies should be asking themselves if their products and services, environmental stance, and corporate practices are consonant with opinion leaders' expectations. What the opinion leaders say and think about companies has more of an impact on what their customers are thinking and doing than companies realize.

PART 3

Planning Modules of the Marcom Engine

9 The Audit Module

This chapter and the following two will discuss the planning modules of the Marcom Engine, and what they can do for you.

The Marcom Audit: What It Can Do for You

Consider the following scenarios:

Zenith Data Systems had a major internal communications problem. First, there was lack of cohesiveness among the many organizations, both internal and external, required to support ZDS, and second there was evidence that the company was no longer sufficiently responsive to the needs of either their distributors or their customers. Bill Davidow, formerly with HP, says in his book *Marketing High Technology*, "Until every single employee understands that the objective of the company is to serve the customer, the customer will never get the best the company can offer." For me it took a seven-month audit of forty-two key employees, from the CEO on down, and a visit to every sales office in the US, Canada, and Australia to analyze the problem and prepare the recommendations.

Silvon Software on the other hand had problems with its external marketing communications. A short audit quickly revealed graphics standards inconsistencies which contributed to an unprofessional image, and evidence of conflicting product messages being sent to the public. Silvon's ads simply lacked focus and failed to talk to the market with a single voice.

Both these issues, one very widespread and the other very specific, were successfully addressed by a Marcom Audit, the first planning module in the Marcom Engine.

What Is A Marcom Audit?

A Marcom Audit is really the first crucial step towards achieving communications power. It enables the persuasive penetration of your product's audience through application of the Marcom Engine, a process approach to marketing communications designed to lend wings to your marketing and spurs to your sales.

Simply stated, the most powerful communication is the simplest. It makes a single statement with a strong emotional appeal. Extraneous information is stripped away so that the promise the product or service makes is sharply in focus.

To achieve this focus, marketers must concentrate their efforts in acquiring knowledge and understanding of their customers' needs, real and perceived, and of their language.

One caution: The viewpoint from which this knowledge will be drawn is as important as the accuracy, and while information will be drawn from a wide range of highly sophisticated sources, THE VIEWPOINT MUST REMAIN THAT OF THE CUSTOMER.

Decisions made as a result of changes in attitude and beliefs on the part of customers are primarily triggered by emotional appeals, which are then quickly rationalized, or justified by the application of logic. But these changes, either in beliefs or behavior, are always done in the CUSTOMER'S TERMS.

Integrated direct marketing offers a tactical approach to concentrating one's communications forces for greater impact. A very simple and ancient analogy demonstrates this point: Imagine picking up a hammer and a nail. Now, instead of driving the nail into a piece of wood point, first reverse it. Pounding on the point in an effort to drive the large flat head of the nail into the wood is what many business-to-business marketers are doing today. Maybe not so blatantly as this illustration, but anytime the messages or actions of your marketing communications are inconsistent with one another, you are attempting to penetrate the mind of your audience using the head of the nail rather than the point.

Developing a program of integrated seamless communications is the methodology whereby we squeeze every last bit of latent energy out of our communications efforts. And the Marcom Audit shows you your current position on the ladder toward successful communications.

Why not resolve to do it *right* this year?

We're talking first about QUALITY of your message and its impact on your marketing communications, and second the MARCOM AUDIT, the way you check up on your quality. In today's quality-conscious world, "getting it done *right*" has finally become more important than simply "getting it done."

Just as on the shop floor or in your development labs, survival today demands continuous improvement in the performance of your marketing activities, especially those communications functions that affect sales, lead generation, market awareness, and shortened selling cycles. To quote Peter Drucker, America's foremost management authority, "That which is measured, improves." That's where a Marcom Audit comes in.

Audits Generate Planning Insights

Over fifty years ago John Wanamaker, the father of modern marketing, was supposed to have said that half of his advertising budget was wasted. His problem was that he did not know which half.

If you suspect that half your advertising dollars are being wasted but are unsure which half, you need a Marcom Audit and then you need to apply corrective action. After correcting the communications deficiencies identified by the marcom audit, what benefits can you expect to achieve?

- Eliminate waste of both time and materials in the production of marketing services deliverables.

- Improve productivity of your ad agency, your in-house marcom support, your ads, collateral, PR, packaging, promotions, etc.

- Sharpen the competitive edge of your sales support activities.

- Increase the reach/frequency of your ad messages with no increase in cost.

- Achieve greater penetration and expand awareness of your message market.

- Most important of all, an effective program of integrated seamless communications will improve your advertising ROI and reduce sales costs.

The EXTERNAL Audit

The external Marcom Audit is a review of your marketing communications, every single facet of it, from top to bottom! Not just advertising, but PR, your web site, email marketing, packaging, collateral, trade show displays, products, corporate ID, direct mail, telemarketing, etc. The Audit searches for inconsistencies in message and appearance. It searches for a lack of focus and continuity between what's promised and what's delivered. Most of all, it seeks to determine if the company is speaking with one voice, and whether the perception by the market matches the perception of management. And following this analysis, it offers suggestions for repairing weak links in the total communications chain.

The INTERNAL Audit

An opening statement by Thomas Perkins, formerly with Hewlett-Packard, (taken from William Davidow's book *Marketing High Technology*) sets the stage for the INTERNAL MARCOM AUDIT: "Many years ago, I found myself managing a computer business ... and loving the challenge, but frustrated by the brutal competition from my sixteen sister divisions for marketing and other resources. The internal competitors made the external competitors, DEC and Data General, look mild."

The Internal Marcom Audit, if successful, will uncover the ways in which people are unconsciously, and with no malice aforethought, aiding and abetting the competition.

Ultimately the goal of the internal Marcom Audit is to identify obstacles to the communications process among employees and vendors. Misunderstandings and communication breaks, which cloud a shared vision, need to be corrected. A detailed analysis of every communications device, every marketing attitude, and every bit of customer-related knowledge will be performed, and the relationships among all departmental entities will be documented, studied, and crossexamined for processes that should be eliminated and those in need of repair. It's important that a simple, focused understanding of the product's promise to its users be clearly understood by every employee, as well as that everyone have a clear picture of the image the company wants to project in the marketplace.

30 Reasons Why You Need Internal and External Audits

1. Improve your marketing ROI.

2. Enhance the impact of your marcom.

3. Extend your ad message's reach and frequency without extending the budget.

4. Reduce wasted time and materials in producing marketing services deliverables.

5. Improve ad agency productivity

6. Improve in-house marcom productivity.

7. Sharpen the competitive edge of sales support activities.

8. Reduce substantially the production costs associated with new creative efforts.

9. Achieve greater message penetration.

10. Expand the awareness of your communications.

11. Tighten the focus of your communications and minimize confusion over your products positioning.

12. Form the basis for a total program of integrated seamless communications.

13. Develop a clear understanding of which parts of your current marcom program are effective and which are not.

14. Form the basis for total marcom tool accountability.

15. Strengthen and achieve better focus for Influencer Relations.

16. Identify inconsistencies between graphics, message, and your company's mission statement.

17. Locate breaks in communications continuity between promises made and products delivered.

18. Determine if the market's perceptions of your company matches management's perception.

19. Detect weaknesses in marcom skills

20. Provide a visual/verbal checklist, or set of standards against which to measure future marcom efforts.

21. Simplify the monitoring of communications activities.

22. Encourage you to probe deeper into your customer's needs, both real and perceived, and to communicate in their language.

23. Force you to sharpen or develop a deliverable positioning strategy.

24. Suggest rethinking your company/marketing missions and to consider bottoms up marketing vs. the traditional top down.

25. Help you treat marketing warfare as if your company's life depended on it.

26. Locate weaknesses in your present communications which may suggest a more serious approach to competitive intelligence.

27. Demand that a comprehensive communications support plan, be developed ASAP.

28. Appreciate the need to understand and reach various audience levels simultaneously.

29. Form the basis for your media strategy.

30. Help achieve a balance between long-term and short-term communications needs.

10 The Strategy Module

The Strategy Module: What It Can Do for You

Consider the following scenarios:

For **KPMG** Peat Marwick Advanced Technologies (Catalyst), my ad agency (KBA) changed their positioning strategy and doubled sales in one year, moving from $3 million to $6 million. **J. D. Edwards** & Company hit a plateau at about $15 million and remained there for many years until KBA presented them to their publics in a different light. With a reenergized sales effort they climbed from $15 to $30 to $45 and on to $60 million over the next three years. Today they're a billion-dollar company owned by Oracle. **Professional Computer Resources** (PCR), after adopting the Bates' A.I.M. (Accelerated Integral Marketing) program doubled sales every year for three years, climbing from $2 million to $4 to $8 and then $16 million. The company was subsequently sold to Pansophic Systems (now owned by **Computer Associates**). **IBM** hired KBA to develop a marcom strategy for the re-launch of

DB2, which contributed a "meaningful impact" to their $8 billion in software sales (actual numbers were proprietary). BCS (**Boeing**) landed Dow Chemical in less than a week following a new ad launch managed by KBA.

Marketing Plans and Communications Plans

Defining terms is a critical first step in the development of a Communications Support Plan. So as to minimize confusion between Marketing Plans and Communications Plans, each is detailed in the following paragraphs:

Marketing Plans cover sales, service, communications, production, pricing, and distribution with subset issues which include research, training, R&D, acquisitions, and facilities planning.

Communications Plans however cover exclusively the communications needs of the marketing plan and focus on such issues as the marketing environment, objectives, strategies, audience targeting, product positioning, market positioning, functional support, communications objectives and strategies, key message, communications flow chart, reach and frequency, communications distribution, accountability, scheduling, funding, depen-dencies, database development, calculating lifetime value, share of mind, database versatility. The Marcom Engine Strategy Module addresses communications planning. The Communications Support Plan (CSP) covers the entire spectrum of going to market.

BENEFITS OF THE STRATEGY MODULE:

- In-depth understanding of market and prospects.

- Building a comprehensive prospect profile.
- A focus on communications tactics.
- More precise market/audience targeting.
- Enhanced product/market positioning.
- An unassailable communications message.
- Budget detail levels that ease funding demands.
- Database development that accelerates one-on-one marketing.
- Improvements in measured media response.
- Differentiate company... more than simple product differentiation.
- A customer marketing communications plan

COMMON PROBLEMS TO BE SOLVED... AND SYMPTONS OF HOW THEY CAN BE RECOGNIZED

1. Cost of sales too high: Symptoms are skewed financial ratios; margins too thin to reach profit goals.

2. Target market/audiences not adequately defined: Symptoms are market segments not being reached; unqualified leads.

3. Product visibility too low: Symptoms include low RFP activity levels; in-adequate lead flow.

4. Budget needs unclear: Symptoms are: poorly defined lead requirements; incomplete media strategy; unfamiliarity with marcom tools; ignorance of industry wide media channel allocations.

5. Weak media integration: Symptoms include lack of media strategy, flow chart, or the presence of a diversified marcom arsenal.

6. Cloudy creative strategy: Symptoms include lack of focus; message inconsistent with mission statement or communications objectives; no clear target individual.

7. Inadequate database: Symptoms include: no source documentation; shallow se-lection criteria; complete update more than 6 months old.

THE PROCEDURE:

ASSEMBLE REFERENCES including all audit material, market research data, independent studies, and both the company's business plan and its marketing plan.

GATHER INTELLIGENCE by interviewing all key people in the organization particularly those closest to the customer such as sales and customer support.

PERFORM ANALYSIS by studying all the material and weighing the company's ambitions against their marketing communications collateral and messages.

PREPARE RECOMMENDATIONS by writing the Communications Support Plan, a document that typically runs from 30 to 90 pages.

Why go to all this trouble? To quote from Ted Leavitt, the Harvard professor who wrote *The Marketing Imagination*, "The purpose of a business is to create and keep a customer. No enterprise, no matter how small can do any of this by mere instinct or accident. It has to clarify its purposes, strategies, and plans, and the larger the enterprise, the greater the necessity that these be clearly written down, clearly communicated, and frequently reviewed by the senior members of the enterprise."

TYPICAL DELIVERABLES FROM MARKETING:

- A marketable vision/mission statement
- A marketing plan audit
- Market Demand/Competitive Claims matrices
- Audience/Ad Vehicle Chart
- Positioning Analysis
- Communications Strategy
- A comprehensive Communications Support Plan with creative, budgeting, and media details

How "whys" men solve marcom strategy challenges.

To construct a marcom strategy, we can return to the Five Whys idea developed at Toyota. This problem-solving technique is a very effective way of delving deeply into your challenges.

Try it, you'll like it! It's incredibly productive and fun to do. And while it evolved as a tool for lean manufacturing, it is equally potent as a process for improving marcom efficiency.

The system is based on all individuals in the sales and marketing process taking responsibility for calling attention to flaws in efficiency or in the metrics that impact ROMS (Return On Marketing Spend) and collaborating on a solution by asking "why" at least 5 times.

To turn yourself into a "whys" man or woman, simply define your current marketing challenge, whether inadequate lead flow, low return on marcom materials, or lack of a clear point person for outside assistance, and structure a question that will lead to the root cause of the problem. In reality you may require anywhere from 3 to 10 answers, but 5 has become the standard.

I stumbled over the process in a book written by William Davidow and Michael Malone titled *The Virtual Corporation*. Davidow's world was technology marketing as VP Sales and Marketing for Intel, and then marketing manager for HP. Malone is the author of *The Big Score*, a highly respected history of the electronics revolution. At the time of the book my ad agency had been immersed in marketing for the software industry for over 15 years, so I found the process most enlightening.

What inspired me to try it for myself was the renewed interest by the technology world in this potent process for uncovering marketing inefficiencies.

To quote *Six Sigma*, "By repeatedly asking the question 'why' (five is a good rule of thumb), you can peel away the layers of symptoms which can lead to the root cause of a problem. Very often the ostensible reason for a problem will lead you to another question. Although this technique is called '5 Whys,' you may find that you need to ask the question fewer or more times than five before you find the issue related to a problem."

What can the 5 Whys do for you?

- Locate the root cause, not simply the symptoms of a problem.
- Provide you with a simple, non-analytic procedure
- Help to define correlations between differing root causes.

What situations respond best to this process?

- Challenges that are based on people interactions.
- Business productivity issues, but not necessarily Six Sigma-related.

5 Whys examples

PROBLEM STATEMENT: (relative to lead *quality*) Neither Sales nor Management is satisfied with the *quality of leads* being generated by Marketing, but there's *no money to expand* the effort. *(Maybe someone should examine the skill levels being applied)*

1. WHY are so few quality leads being generated for the sales force?	Because the present marcom efforts seem to be performing poorly.
2. WHY are the present marcom efforts performing poorly?	Because the creative strategy doesn't seem up to the task of changing the attitudes that lead to changes in behavior within our target market.
3. WHY isn't the creative strategy stimulating responses from the right people?	Because it was prepared by people who are not grounded in the development of creative strategies.
4. WHY was work given to people without the necessary background skills?	Because it was assumed that the expertise possessed by our marketing staff would be adequate.
5. WHY was this assumption made?	Because it was always adequate in the past. And our ad agency should have been able to supply the necessary creative skills.

PROBLEM STATEMENT: (relative to *lead costs*) Neither Sales nor Management is satisfied with the *quality of leads* being generated by Marketing but there's *no money to expand* the efforts. *(Maybe someone should revisit where the money goes)*

1. WHY are so few quality leads being generated for the sales force?	Because we are not spending marketing money in the right places.
2. WHY aren't we spending money in the right places?	Because we have a flawed creative strategy.
3. WHY do we have a flawed creative strategy?	Because no one on staff seems to have the level of skills required to build a strategy with any assurance of success.
4. WHY don't we have access to the skills we need?	Because management doesn't seem to place enough credence on marketing strategy and creative execution, and is reluctant to allow hiring a consultant.
5. WHY this seeming reluctance to get the help that's needed?	Because of the perception that hiring outside creative help is very expensive and requires an ongoing commitment.

Take-Away Quotation (from *Six Sigma*)

"If you don't ask the right questions, you don't get the right answers. A question asked in the right way often points to its own answer. Asking questions is the ABC of diagnosis. Only the inquiring mind solves problems." – Edward Hodnett

Because this book is designed to be *useful* in addition to being *enlightening,* I've enclosed the following two charts to help with both communications and marketing planning. This process evolved from my work with ad agency giant Wells Rich & Greene as part of my efforts for client IBM.

QUICKCHEK COMMUNICATIONS STRATEGY STATEMENT (preliminary)

A. Purpose: The Strategy Statement evolves from the blending of Audit and Strategy information and is done as a guide to development within the Creative module. Its' purpose is simply to raise awareness of issues important to the creative. The "final" Strategy Statement must await completion of the Communications Support Plan.

B. "QuickChek", fill-in-the-blanks exercise: The target individual, by title, is the ____. Whose specific buying role is (economic, technical, or end user) ____. His/her specific current behavior as it relates to us is ____. Because he/she currently believes that ____. Therefore, this communications effort must confront this person's existing feelings so that his/her new beliefs will be ____. So that the person will be more likely to have this specific new behavior ____.

Below is a sample form with keys to the info required.

Audience:	Identify primary target audience individuals only for this exercise.
Problem:	State the problem for which your product or service offers a solution *from the buyers perspective only*. Determine the degree to which you are filling a need that's already being met. Be careful you're not offering a solution for which there is not a clearly defined problem. Examine evidence that says the market wants your solution strong enough to desert others already filling the gap, though perhaps inadequately. Is your solution worthy of viral marketing?
Marcom Objective:	Restate who you are trying to reach and what you are trying to persuade them to believe so as to change present buying habits.
Marcom Strategy:	What position are you going to take to differentiate your product/service, and what tactics are you going to employ, to reach and persuade your target audience.
Marcom Tactics	Tactical launch sequence: viral/influencers to regular hubs, press releases to mega hubs, and accelerated contagion to sustain the word of mouth
Message Support:	What specific reasons to believe, evidence, incentives can you use to create new beliefs? What can you show, demonstrate, provide as "news" etc. i.e., "Why should our prospect change beliefs, and subsequently his buying behavior?"
Desired Response:	Sum up, in a short sentence, the reaction we would like to get from our target audience upon experiencing our communications.

Required Mentions:	List major users, key reference companies, recent major press issues, testimonials, etc.
Competition	List primary competitors, or those perceived by your prospect to be competitors, or alternative solutions to the one your offer. List URLs.

QUICKCHEK MARKETING STRATEGY STATEMENT (preliminary) Chasm Companion

A. Purpose: The Strategy Statement evolves from the blending of Audit and Strategy information and is done as a guide to development within the Creative module. Its' purpose is simply to raise awareness of issues important to the creative. The "final" Strategy Statement must await completion of the Communications Support Plan.

B. "QuickChek", fill-in-the-blanks exercise: The target individual, by title, is the ____. Whose specific buying role is (economic, technical, or end user) ____. His/her specific current behavior as it relates to us is ____. Because he/she currently believes that ____. Therefore, this communications effort must confront this person's existing feelings so that his/her new beliefs will be ____. So that the person will be more likely to have this specific new behavior ____.

Below is a sample form with keys to the info required.

Target Customer:	High-tech target customer sets typically comprise an economic buyer, a technical buyer, and an end user. Each group asserts its influence to different points on the TALC (Technical Adoption Life Cycle).
Compelling Reason to Buy:	To build an effective strategy you must understand in detail the target customer's motivation to buy. These motivations change over the course of the TALC.
Whole Product Analysis:	This comprises the minimum set of products and services need to fulfill the target customer's compelling reason to buy.
Partners, Allies, Relationships:	These groups represent anyone outside the chief sponsor of the whole product who can play a potential role in creating, delivering, and/or endorsing the whole product.
Distribution:	Two principals govern what distribution method should be chosen to sell, deploy, and support a new product: *solution complexity* and *marketing complexity*.
Pricing:	Pricing models shift over the Technology Adoption Life cycle as business models change.
Competitive Environment:	Competitive positions typically reflect two sets: *reference* competition, a set of alternatives that reflect an overall position (benefit and differentiation); and *economic* competition, a set of alternatives that compete for a customer's budget.

Positioning:	This element refers to asserting and occupying an advantageous position within two systems: the first is the system of *buying choices* that the target customer may consider; the second is the systems or *partners and allies* that constitute a given value chain in the marketplace. (not to be confused with Trout/Ries original positioning concepts)
Next Target:	Literally the next customer, this element is based on the inflection point and market development model appropriate to each phase of the TALC.

11 The Creativity Module

The Creativity Module: What It Can Do for You

Consider the following scenarios:

To generate 1000 leads at $500 per lead will cost you $500,000. However, to generate 1000 leads at $200 per lead will only cost $200,000. By dropping the cost per lead only 60% you saved $300,000. How can you drop the cost per lead while still getting the message out? By redesigning your messaging whether to suit word of mouth scripting or website or email or direct mail, etc., so that marcom efforts currently pulling 20 leads per effort pull 50. That's all. You didn't change the product. You didn't change the price. You simply presented it to your market in a better light. A two-and-one-half times improvement can save you over a quarter-million dollars.

Consider the case of the direct marketer living on telesales supported by leads. He sells 1000 units at $600 each, but lead costs consume $500, leaving a margin of about 17%. By dropping the cost per lead only 60% margins leap 50%. All you have to do is redesign the campaign that is pulling 20 leads per thousand (2%) to pull 50 leads per thousand (5%). How can you get results like these? Invest in the Creativity Module of the Marcom Engine! We have often improved leads not just by the 250% above, but by 500% to 1000% depending on the state of the market and the client's value proposition.

The Ultimate Differentiator

I have been a student of the creative process for over 50 years and can share the key steps with you. As part of our Marcom Engine we developed the Creative Repository concept, incorporating Core Intelligence from the Audit and Strategy modules plus theme/image standards which evolve from the application of creative skills. This repository becomes the basis for all marketing and branding communications for the company and its products.

The Creativity module, third and last module of the Marcom Engine planning process, consists of two key components: core intelligence and theme/image standards. These make up the mixing bowl where the ingredients provided by the audit and strategy modules become core intelligence, and are blended with raw creative power to produce THE BIG IDEA (lightning bolt) which is the source of all communications energy and the basis for our theme/image standards.

This is where "big ideas" are developed for your communications execution, and I'd like to share with you the creative process. Marcom planning and producing are great, but without the "big idea" you're only halfway there. Technology marketing is a special challenge to the creative effort because of the diversity of benefits and the complex audience matrix involved. To succeed we look for messages with stopping power, but not at the sacrifice of relevancy to both product and corporate branding issues. To quote David Ogilvy, famed founder and creative head of Ogilvy & Mather advertising, "You can do your homework from now until doomsday, but you will never win fame and fortune unless you also invent big ideas."

Probing the Mystery of Creativity

The creative process is launched by mixing core intelligence with text and imagery to populate the Marcom Engine with BIG IDEA elements. Most marcom graphics are too complex. Simple icons work best. The generally accepted creative process follows these steps.

- **PREPARATION (inform)** Mastery of subject matter
- **INCUBATION (explore)** Relax, Free Association, Visualization, Scanning
- **ILLUMINATION (~)** Lightning bolt arrives if environment is OK
- **ELABORATION (judge)** Return to analytical state, arrange, expand, edit
- **VERIFICATION (build)** Test, refine, submit for approval

The Marcom Engine will help you become a marketing communications genius ... but do you have the right stuff to become a *creative* genius?

Because creativity consists in rearranging existing knowledge, you must allow yourself to explore the connections among your various interests and pursuits. The more widely these connections range, the richer they can be. My lifestyles include those of an artist, musician, writer, mountain climber, licensed pilot, licensed African professional hunter, entrepreneur of five corporations, and father to four incredible daughters. You must also possess ONE of the following two sets of personal traits: wholesome, confident, perceptive, charismatic – or – driven, uneasy, remote, sometimes neurotic. Plus you must possess ALL the following character traits:

- a tolerance of ambiguity, disorder, tension, and conflict
- a desire to create new order from disorder
- an ability to stand fast with personal visions and ideas in the face of group pressure.

Studies indicate that creativity and brilliant intellect do not fit snugly together: creative people have moderate to high intelligence, but neither a phenomenally high IQs nor a spectacular memory are prerequisites for creativity.

Why does the Marcom Engine preach integrated marketing communications?

Because repetition of emotion-evoking messages is the only known way to assure penetration of the belief clusters that serve as cognitive dissonance filters. Because message retention is dependent on the use of a variety of input vehicles. And because pictures are far superior to words when it comes to altering the brain chemistry required for both penetration and retention. So if you're contemplating a boring visual or an all-copy message, you're in trouble

These revelations resulted from work in neuroscience by Charlene Swansea and grew into her book *Mindworks*, which is one of my all-time favorites. It was published in 1990 by South Carolina ETV.

The challenge for creativity is to overpower, or alter, ingrained beliefs (sometimes referred to as the bullshit factor)

The real target of our efforts is not defined demographically (statistics), or psychographically (lifestyles) or even synchrographically (timing). The target is the brain and the challenge is to change attitudes, which in turn change behavior. Attitude changes occur through changes in brain chemistry, so think of yourself as a chemist, working on penetration and retention.

The paradox: The quirky unknown doesn't stick unless you successfully help your reader relate it to the known. The four most feared words in marketing communications? I DON'T BELIEVE YOU!

One of today's biggest obstacles to sales...

...and to the efficiency of the marketing that drives it is resistance to migration from the status quo. The Random Task approach to sales and marketing communications, common over the past decade, just isn't good enough anymore when introducing consumers to new ideas. The solution today is to embrace the hottest new marketing paradigm since the technology market implosion of 2000—the concept of word of mouth marketing and its application to the various social media!

Communications professionals know it's not what you say about your product, but how you say it that counts. Focus, clarity, positioning, objectivity. Constructing a creative and effective word of mouth marketing scheme can be a challenge, but once you have one, you'll never look back!

For examples of creative work done for KBA clients over the past 30 years visit:

http://www.kbates.com/images/THE_AD_PORTFOLIO.pdf

Benefits of the Creativity Module:

- Substantial reductions in the cost of sales.

- Reduction of dependency on field sales support.

- Reduction of selling cycles by 20% to 50%;

- Improved impact of your marketing dollars, often by 200% or more!

Problems to Be Solved:

- Low market awareness

- Many unqualified leads

- Low response rates

- Selling cycles too long

- Weak brand equity

- Cost of leads too high,

- Poor positioning relative to competitors

Specifics of Problems to Be Solved ...
And How They Can Be Recognized

1. Low market awareness and the perception of an identity crisis. Symptoms include loosing sales to lesser quality products from highly visible competitors. Confusion in market caused by conflicting competitive claims/market demand.

2. Time/money wasted on unqualified leads. Symptoms are queries indicating poor comprehension of your marketing communication, failure to fit profile of a receptive prospect.

Message doesn't fit the audience probably as a result of failing to build an audience/ad vehicle matrix.

3. Ads, mailers seem to lack focus. Response rates are low. Symptoms are communications pieces loaded with all possible product attributes in an effort to be all things to all people. Failure to put emphasis on single point of market-desired differentiation. Message inconsistency.

4. Selling cycles too long due to lack of clarity in ads. Prospects enter cycle at wrong time. Symptoms are a blur of complex technical features either unrelated or poorly connected to user oriented benefits. Failure to poll sufficient numbers of customers/prospects to deter-mine their most critical needs.

5. Weak Unique Selling Proposition (USP). Company not putting its best foot forward. Symptoms are evidence that core competency not clearly defined. Cloudy message.

6. Cost of sales/leads going up. Symptoms are low response, lead flow, resulting from boring messages, weak, uninspired headlines and graphics. Misdirected messages. Company fails to understand the position occupied in the market's mind and has no creative strategy that responds.

7. Loosing business to parity products. Symptoms include poor brand equity. Poor positioning strategy. Low levels of market awareness.

Great thoughts on creativity by giants of the advertising industry.

This contribution comes from Tom Hall of Ogilvy & Mather
BEWARE OF TAMING THE LIGHTNING OF A GREAT IDEA

Lightning is a metaphor for two contrasting experiences: sudden illumination and sudden death. Ben Franklin tamed the sudden death aspect. He gave us lightning rods so that we could admire the light without fearing the consequences. Sudden illumination is not a new phenomenon to marketers. Many a competitor has grabbed the lead with a brilliant marketing ploy... but more often brilliant ideas die with barely a whimper because of human lightning rods ... people with a knack for grounding great ideas ... people uncomfortable with change/new ideas... people who fear a burst of inspiration will wipe out the way they've been doing things, people who don't want the bright light of your BIG IDEA to make theirs look dim by comparison. Be patient with lightning rods. And be prepared to use the irrefutable logic made possible by the MARCOM ENGINE.

And this contribution comes from Charlotte Beers, also of Ogilvy & Mather

WHY OUTSOURCE YOUR CREATIVE STRATEGY?

Charlotte Beers of Ogilvy and Mather said it best in this excerpt from a speech she gave many years ago... "What do ad agencies do that's unique?"

Let me suggest that the people in advertising are deliberately, joyfully, urgently different from our clients, not better, different ... We do offer something to clients they can't get elsewhere. We are people you could never hire, for ideas you could never have.

Conversely, our clients have a kind of mastery we don't have. They take risks, have great drive, thoroughness to make it happen, ensure against failure, scope and scale for our ideas.

We match mastery with inspiration ... all the "I" words; ideas, imagination, insight, and intuition. If clients are in charge of the linear logical world of common sense, we are responsible for uncommon sense. In thousands of offices allover the country, clients are saying in meetings with their agency - Well, I hadn't thought of it that way... Clients see people as consumers first, we "see" consumers as people first. The most successful clients, the most profitable clients have a profound appreciation of our differences.

Companies organize people, product and profit. Agencies organize ideas. It is the duty of the former to protect the power of the latter. It does take a different culture to nourish idea people, we need a place where we can entertain visions, a place where we can keep fantasy, ridicule and doubt alive and well. **It's passion that makes an agency**.

Next up, the Marcom Engine Charts*

On the following two pages you will find two charts that present a very simple overview of the six modules that make up the Marcom Engine. The preceding chapters have explored the Planning modules. The next three chapters will take you through the Execution modules.

*SAMPLE MARCOM ENGINE CHART

PLANNING

AUDITING Product, Market, and Competitors	STRATEGY Market Development Checklist	CREATIVE Positioning within a system of choices

Primary Market Research / Surveys on mVerify prospects
- instantsurvey.com
- surveymonkey.com
- zoomerang.com
- Global Market Insite
- Greenfield Online

Secondary Market Research on Mobile Testing
- Gartner.com
- Forrester.com
- Aberdeen
- Yankee Group
- Competitors White Papers

Communications Audit: External – to determine if company speaking to market with one voice. Critical for marcom efforts.

Communications Audit: Internal – to determine if there are breaks in the shared vision. Critical for channel marketing.

CHECKLIST: Target Customer
- VP Operations
- VP Quality
- VP of Engineering

Compelling reason to buy
- Dramatically reduces time to market

Whole Product:
- Automated testing tools
- Conversion from manual
- Script library maint.

Partners and allies
- Symbol, HP, Dell, DAP
- ActiveState Tcl, MySql
- QA Mgr. evaluates
- Procurement buys

Distribution Channels
- Direct download
- Dongle

Pricing
- Per Seat bundle
- $25k-$50k
- Team edition coming
- Enterprise edition too

Competition
- TestQuest
- Mobile Complete
- Bug Huntress
- Internally developed

Positioning
- Relative to competition
- Within the prospects mind

The Creative Process
- Overview

Creative Elements
- Influencer Relations & Evangelism
- Viral Marketing
- Accelerated Contagion
- Sales Support

Copy Platform
Development in support of Competitive Differences between other mobile testing products:
- Mobile Testing Nightmare
- Now available Scalable
- Slow to market
- Automated app testing

Theme/Image standards:
- Theme: Copy development per messaging process
- Image: Graphics development per Bates 5-step process

Market Specific Messaging
- Mfrs. mobile devices
- ISVs mobile apps
- US Govt. DOD users
- Carriers (Verizon, etc)
- ASPs, SaaS
- Enterprise IT

EXECUTION

ARSENAL Resources for distribution	**DEPLOYMENT** Word of Mouth Marketing Processes	**MEASUREMENT** Measurement Metrics and ROI Tracking

Collateral
- Trade shows materials
- Website Development
- SEO, SEM
- Seminars
- Webinars
- Testimonials
  - Case studies
  - Corporate brochure
  - Weblog (possibly)
  - Newsletter (definitely)
  - Competitor guidebook
  - Inbound call scripting

Marketing Database
- List Development
- Database Mgmt.

SalesForceAutomation
- Salesforce.com

Web Analytics
- Email analysis
- Relationship analysis

Search Engine Optimize
- Free search based on appeal to spiders
- Monthly Maint. Reqd.

Search Engine Marketing
- Paid search based on bidding with major search engines (Google/Yahoo, etc.)

Event Marketing Experiential Marketing

Influencer Relations
Traditional PR Model
- Media
- Analysts
- Industry Experts

Influentials Model

Mega Hubs
- Analysts
- Elite Media: Trade/Bus.
- Industry gurus
- Industry Associations

Regular Hubs
- Customers
- Academics
- Partners
- Govt. / Legislature
- Groups / Orgs
- Trade writers/authors
- Detractors
- Evangelists

Viral Marketing/Seeding
- 30 second videos
- Email marketing
- Customer Evangelists
- New Tech
- Network Hubs (Mavens, etc.)
- Blogs, Newsgroups, CGM (Consumer Generated Media) now known as Social Media

Accelerated Contagion
- Integrated DM
- Telemarketing
- Mailing Fulfillment
- Print media
- Webinars
- Trade shows
- Seminars

Channel Support

Measuring marketing impact of Word of Mouth episodes (per WOMMA):
- Consumptions: message received- no action taken.
- Inquiries: seeks more info after consumption.
- Conversions: receiver completes desired action.
- Relays: receiver redistributes the message
- Re-Creations: receiver creates new WOM unit after consumption of initial one.

Traditional Media watching
- www.bzzagent.com
- www.technorati.com
- www.blogpulse.com

Traditional Media analysis
- Nielsen-online.com
- Attensity.com
- www.Cymphony.com

Social Media Listening
- Alerts.google.com
- Socialmention.com
- Whostalkin.com
- Attensity.com
- Technorati.com
- Twitterati.com
- Blogpulse.com

Social Media Analysis
- Howsociable.com
- Backtype.com
- Trendistic.com
- Hootsuite.com
- Raventools, com
- Peerindex.net
- Cymfony.com

Execution Modules of the Marcom Engine

12 The Arsenal Module

The Arsenal Module: Converting intangibles to tangibles!

B rilliant ideas are elusive. Before being shared with your market they must achieve substance. Yesterday this was easy. You simply turned your messaging concepts over to an artist, writer, or your ad agency and they turned them into ads or brochures or postcards or a direct mail piece. Today life is not so simple.

Today, the internet has changed everything, and arsenal options include white papers, websites, microsites, SEO (search engine optimization), SEM (search engine marketing), seminars, webinars, blogs, PowerPoints, case studies, broadcast voicemail, podcasts and online newsletters, Facebook, Twitter, LinkedIn, and YouTube as well as yesterday's brochures, direct mail, and trade show booths and materials..

On top of all these media are valuable services ranging from database management to CRM (with SalesForce.com leading the pack) and email marketers. And don't forget to learn about web analytics, data mining, and predictive analytics as well.

Beware: "integrated marketing" has two meanings

Endless books have been written on the concept of integrated marketing communications. The term "integrated" confuses some people in that it seems to have two meanings. One meaning stresses the importance of integrating *media* so as to create the repetition that makes your messaging stick. However, that is more of a deployment issue to be addressed in the next chapter. The meaning we are concerned with in this chapter is that of integrated *creativity,* so that all your marketing materials appear to have originated from the same company and promote a single value proposition. It seems like a relatively simple concept and not terribly difficult to execute... but not many people do it. This is where the discipline of the theme/image process within the Creative module becomes very important.

Back to the Creative Module for a Moment

In the Creative module we formed the words and pictures that we felt best represented what we sell by settling on a single thought and a single graphic. In the Arsenal module we are now faced with the challenge of taking a single theme and applying it to multiple formats. Some of these formats, podcasting for example, won't allow any graphics, while others such as product brochures will require that you extend the graphic feel without destroying the consistency. If you find this difficult to do you may want to revisit your theme/image standards.

One approach I frequently use is to start with what appears to be a full page ad in a trade publication – even though your media strategy dictates that you have no use for an ad. What's valuable is the discipline required to force your words and pictures into a clearly defined framework, typically 8 ½" x 11". When you have explored all possible creative approaches and received management's approval, it becomes relatively easy to apply the creative concept to any shape or size ranging from truck posters to websites.

One of the major issues of the Arsenal module is the arsenal strategy, not to be confused with the deployment strategy. Questions to be considered in forming an arsenal strategy are precisely what marcom tools will you need, and what kind of budget is available to support that decision. The range of possibilities is fairly dramatic, reaching from inexpensive postcards to often costly search engine marketing. While SEM is certainly a critical consideration, more and more CEOs and CMOs I talk to are starting to take SEO more seriously and adopting an attitude of getting their house (website) in order before displaying it to the world.

13 The Deployment Module

Deploying Your Arsenal

When it comes time to *deploy* your arsenal, you have to choose to use either individually, or in combination, from a list of media vehicles that runs the gamut from websites (optimized or not), microsites, search engines (in a multitude of flavors), blogs, forums, email marketing, voice and fax broadcasting, telemarketing, direct mail, tradeshows, webinars, seminars, print media, broadcast media, outdoor, mobile devices, experiential, promotional, list seeding, social media, and podcasting, not to mention the dozens of ways of formatting messages in support of influencer relations and evangelism.

The four major deployment strategies

Keep in mind that while there are endless tools and a multitude of media to explore, your deployment must be separate, and yet integrated, across the components of your embedded word of mouth program. These key components are influencer relations, viral marketing, accelerated contagion, and frequently channel support.

The growing need for media strategists

For those facing too many media options, you may need access to a media strategist. To quote Kate Maddox of *BtoB Magazine*, "In today's complex marketing environment, which requires innovative strategies to help break through the clutter and realize a return on limited marketing dollars, media strategists have increasingly valuable jobs." Media planners are in high demand partly because of the challenge of working with smaller marketing budgets and because of the need to integrate messages across a range of media from traditional to online.

Developing a media strategy in the complex world of print, broadcast, and broadband can be a little intimidating for the neophyte, and even for the professional. Witness a series of articles run by the Wall Street Journal several years back about the dilemma traditional ad agencies and PR firms are having in coping with dozens of new talent requirements which are sadly lacking on their staff. Be careful to find someone well-versed in digital media.

Excerpts from this WSJ series include headlines and text like:

"MADISON AVENUE is being re-paved. Facing unprecedented upheaval in the advertising and media industries, big ad holding companies and their agency units are rethinking how they're organized. Traditional agencies were built for a world in which glossy print ads and high-priced jazzy TV commercials were the dominant form of marketing.

That's less the case nowadays, as marketers siphon off ad dollars from traditional media to spend on newfangled ad approaches such as word-of-mouth marketing, mobile phones and social media."

"The result? Under pressure from marketers, agencies are starting to re-structure operations by aligning their creative sides with less glamorous parts of their businesses such as marketing services–which include direct mail and in-store advertising–and media-buying and planning. Moreover, with just about everyone eager to increase the use of Web marketing, traditional agencies are quickly snapping up digital marketing firms or hiring experienced digital staffers."

"SOME ARE CALLING it the revenge of the nerds. Soaring demand for online advertising is creating an all-out battle on Madison Avenue for people who can create or sell interactive ads. A shortage of advertising talent with digital-media experience is sending salaries soaring-up as much as 60% in the past year, according to a new survey–and making it hard for some smaller digitally focused ad firms to compete."

"This is not a demand- or a supply- constrained market. It is a human-capital-constrained market. There is more demand for expertise than there is expertise."

"Part of the problem, (from)Yahoo's Ms. Millard, is that skills required in the online- and old-media worlds are so different that few people can easily "toggle back and forth."

"In a sign of how the once-sharp dividing line between the media world and Madison Avenue is disappearing, publisher and broadcaster Meredith Corp. acquired of two interactive-marketing agencies, giving it a significant presence in the ad world."

"We believe the marketing services area will have a faster growth rate than either of the two traditional-media businesses," Mr. Lacy says.

"Marketers are also trying to figure out how much advertising they can place on mobile devices without being rebuffed by consumers."

"Having an outside consultant that can help co-ordinate multiple agencies as they work on a project makes for a compelling alternative, she says.

"You really can't expect a traditional marketing group to really understand and be a champion for the new media," says Jim Smith, chairman and chief executive of Webster Financial, a Waterbury, Conn., financial-services company, another BrightLine client.

Deployment complexity is driving need for single providers

From a *BtoB Magazine* article by Carol Krol titled *Need for leads fuels frenzy of direct deals* comes the following comment, "With an ever-expanding array of media choices, marketing has never been more complex, and marketers are increasingly demanding sophisticated solutions to find customers and deliver relevant messages. In addition, marketers need measurement tools to gauge success and justify budgets in a climate of increased accountability. What has become even more appealing is the prospect of finding end-to-end marketing tools from a single provider."

14 The Measurement Module

The Challenge of Measuring Marketing Effectiveness

Two processes: Word of Mouth, and Traditional.

C urrently on the horizon are two approaches to measurement and metrics of which we must develop a working knowledge. Each has its own terms and metrics. You must become familiar with both, gaining if not expert knowledge then at least a working knowledge sufficient enough to enable you to hire an expert.

Traditional

Almost everyone will agree that the curse of traditional marketing communications is the complexity of measuring its effectiveness either in terms of responses or dollars. Endless books have been written on the topic as well as organizations established to perform analysis. One of the best organizations I've run across in many years is the recently formed CMO Council (www.cmocouncil.org). More than 6,000 members of the Chief Marketing Officer (CMO) Council control well over $200 billion in aggregated annual marketing spend. These include senior corporate marketing leaders and brand decision-makers in 110 countries and across all industries.

Word of Mouth Marketing

The excerpt that follows is courtesy of WOMMA and was taken from their Measurement and Metrics Guidebook published in 2009

Available at: http://wommastore.eventbrite.com/

A new guidebook is scheduled for release in Fall 2011.

Introduction

The promise of word of mouth (WOM) marketing initiatives has practically saturated the consciousness of every brand marketer: relevant, more targeted reach leading to more efficient use of marketing dollars, a virtual focus group providing commentary about a company's products and services, and opportunities for engaging customers in greater dialogue, just to name a few.

But one important barrier to adopting WOM marketing more broadly has been a lack of understanding about what, and how, to measure the impact of WOM marketing. Without this understanding, we lack the ability as marketers to build our business cases, demonstrate the impact of our programs, and have the security and support from upper management to make huge leaps forward.

How We Define Word of Mouth and Social Media

Consistent with WOMMA's Word of Mouth Terminology Framework, we define WOM as the sharing of marketing-relevant information among consumers, and we define WOM marketing as efforts by an organization to encourage, facilitate, and amplify marketing-relevant communication among consumers. Over the past few years the use of "social media" has increased due to the proliferation of various communication technologies and applications that amplify consumer voices and facilitate social relationships, such as blogs and microblogs, social networking sites, video and photo sharing, etc. WOMMA views WOM and social media as related, but not synonymous, terms.

Generally speaking, social media is a sub-set of WOM. More specifically, the relationship between WOM and social media is threefold. First, social media can be understood as online WOM activity. Second, social media is the collection of digital venues in which WOM occurs. Third, social media is an engine or set of tools to achieve WOM marketing goals.

The entries in this Guidebook present metrics that address both online and offline forms of WOM. We have also included a special section on social media success metrics to specifically address measurement frameworks and case studies for marketing campaigns that leverage social media tools to generate WOM and drive trial and sales.

What this Guidebook Is and Is Not

The Guidebook is intended as an educational resource for marketers to better understand metrics and measurement as they relate to word of mouth and social media marketing programs. The following pages offer a broad overview of the types of metrics available, key considerations for their use, and specific examples of their application. It will cover topics such as how to quantify the volume and sentiment of WOM, measure advocacy, determine what a brand-related conversation is worth to the brand's bottom-line, and calculate the ROI of WOM and social media marketing initiatives.

The Guidebook is *not* intended to offer industry standards or a definitive statement on the "one right way" to measure WOM. Standards develop in industries over many years of productive debate and refinement and moving towards standardization too quickly can stifle growth and innovation.

Word of Mouth within the MEASUREMENT Module

Measuring the Impact of WOMM: Measuring the marketing impact of Word of Mouth Marketing becomes the measuring of 'episodes,' according to WOMMA. Episodes are referred to as either Consumptions, in which a message is received but no action taken; Inquiries, in which a receiver seeks more info after consumption; Conversions, in which a receiver completes the desired action; Relays, in which a receiver redistributes the message; or Re-Creations, a situation where a receiver creates a new WOM unit after consumption of the initial one.

Most of my readers will probably need to expand their marketing vocabulary to be effective at WOMM measurement. Fortunately help is close at hand via WOMMA (Word of Mouth Marketing Association) which can be readily found at www.womma.org. Once there you must click on Programs, then on Research and Metrics, then on WOMMA Terminology Framework and then open, or simply turn to

Chapter 15, the Measurement Module. This chapter will give you the terminology you need to get started

As you begin the process of measuring your programs, it is important that you are using both qualitative and quantitative methods of tracking. Tracking just what people are saying, or just counts of followers, will not on their own provide the insights you need. The total picture needs to be developed in a holistic way to develop actionable understanding. The process can be broken down into two key areas, with tools available to help with each.

Social Media Listening: This is the process of tracking who is talking about your organization, and what they are saying about it. Some of the sites and tools available to automate this process include alerts.google.com, socialmention.com, whostalkin.com, www.attensity.com, technorati.com, twitterati.com, and blogpulse.com. More are evolving daily.

Social Media Analysis: Similar to social media listening services these sites also perform measurement of CGM (consumer generated media). There is no fully defined "best practice" on what to track and how, but each service provider has an array of analytics that help to reveal and classify your word of mouth performance metrics. Some of the resources to explore in this space include howsociable.com, backtype.com, trendistic.com, hootsuite.com, raventools.com, peerindex.net and cymfony.com

However, a word of caution: Web watching/listening and web analytics are growing more sophisticated with each passing hour and range from free to very expensive. And, at the same time, while new resources emerge, others are merging and consolidating. Do your homework, but by all means, jump into measurement and analytics and use them to guide your online evolution.

About WOMMA

WOMMA is the official trade association for the word of mouth marketing industry. Our mission is to build a prosperous word of mouth marketing industry based on ethics, best practices, and measurable ROI. Our members are leading the efforts necessary to create a new, successful marketing field. We're growing WOM from a small specialty into an essential part of the marketing mix. We're fantastic brands and marketers who know that happy customers are our most powerful advocates. We're innovative agencies who understand how to empower and amplify the voice of the consumer. And we're the good guys, committed to protecting consumers with strong ethical guidelines.

PART

5

Wrapping It Up in the CSP

15 The Communications Support Plan

The Communications Support Plan: Where It All Comes Together

All the hard work in WOMM and Marcom Engine development now form the blueprint for action.

In the beginning there was ADAPSO, the Association of Data Processing Organizations. Then they became ITAA. Today they're called TechAmerica after merging with AeA, GEIA and CSIA, and represent the largest and strongest voice and resource for technology in the United States. Together, they are the industry's leading trade association, giving the tech sector a strong voice and offering companies a broad array of exceptional programs and services.

ITAA was the organization that fostered the relationship my company developed with the software marketing folks at IBM, leading to a contract to "provide services to IBM which result in a strategic plan and a new positioning concept for a variety of IBM software offerings." This in turn led to my exposure to and subsequent adoption of the Communications Support Plan concept.

The initial agreement went on to say, "The work product on the positioning concept will include a communication plan and examples of prototype communications that verbalize and visualize how this concept could be presented to respective market segments." I developed my version of the Communications Support Plan in response to this need.

How I opened the door at IBM, and met the CSP

It all began when I approached Bob Berland, a friend of mine and a senior VP at IBM, at the conclusion of a speech he gave before an ADAPSO meeting. He died shortly after that meeting, but not before coming to Chicago to study my agency and introduce me to Byron Quann, Director of Marketing Communications for IBM and a great guy to work for.

What prompted his visit was my comment to him after his speech that IBM really didn't understand how to market DB2, their answer to Oracle's introduction of a relational DBMS (database management system). Oracle's product had been on the market for a few years and was really cleaning house as they had virtually no competitors.

I contended that IBM's DB2 launch was flawed

As I recall IBM's offering had been on the market for about six months and was going nowhere. I offered to show them what to do, and was subsequently invited to White Plains for interviewing. During this visit I was offered a copy of a McKinsey study that had been done on the RDBMS market, which I considered seriously flawed, and let this be known to my emerging friends at IBM. Next on the agenda was a visit by several senior IBM execs to my offices in Chicago to interview my employees. This was followed by a nice letter that said in effect, "Your agency is too small to handle IBM but we would like to hire you as a consultant to relaunch DB2." After some conversation I accepted, and so began a wonderful relationship lasting several years.

So I went to work for IBM. My primary contact was Nancy McCrocklin in White Plains, and a lovely lady to work with, very patient with me as I learned the intricacies of working with the world's largest software vendor. In my work I made the rounds and got familiar with their offices in Armonk, Rye, Purchase and White Plains. But White Plains was pretty much home, and I'll never forget my introductory visit...they met me at the airport with a silver Mercedes stretch limousine, the longest limo I had ever seen.

Enter the Communications Support Plan

IBM has a stellar reputation for marketing, and I chose to adapt my ADplan concept of many years to IBM's much more sophisticated process. I have used it, with some modifications, ever since.

White Plains is where Nancy introduced me to the Communications Support Plan, the focus of this closing chapter. She handed me a small booklet titled *In Concert...Marketing and Communications, Bringing a product to market.* I'm not going to burden you with the contents of this twelve page brochure, but the opening paragraphs which follow provides its focus:

Orchestrating a partnership

When you see an eye-catching brochure or an exciting commercial, you can be sure it took lots of people and lots of time to put it together. Positioning the product, developing the marketing program, targeting the audience, crafting the message, and selecting the media is the result of a partnership involving many functions.

In M&SG, that partnership is primarily between Marketing and Communications. Together, we have a common goal–to ensure the effective, affordable, on-time marketing support of IBM products and programs.

This guide's for you

The objective of this guide–written for you, the Marketing sponsor–is to describe the process of developing a Communications Support Plan (CSP). The CSP is the method M&SG uses to develop and execute an effective communications program. You play a critical role in the process, and understanding your responsibilities will help ensure that your product or program gets the support it warrants, whether that's a full-scale campaign for a major product introduction, supporting a new marketing program with selective media, or a single press release announcing an enhancement.

Well before your partnership with Communications begins, you often will be working with other organizations to develop a Marketing Plan for your product or program. The Strategy and Market Analysis organization, for example, can provide marketplace analysis, market research and competitive analysis. The Marketing Plans function can offer planning guidance and other assistance in the development of your Marketing Plan. Some of the information in your Marketing Plan is essential in developing a CSP to support your program.

Preparing a Communications Support Plan can entail up to six basic steps:

1. Program initiation

2. Information input .

3. Documenting the CSP

4. Establishing the communications concept

5. Creative execution and production

6. Measurement and analysis

When the CSP has been completed, it is reviewed and approved by both Marketing and Communications. At this time you can incorporate the CSP into your Market Support Plan. Then, it's show time! That means the Communications functions and the agency do their creative work.

Sample Contents for a
Word of Mouth Marketing
COMMUNICATIONS SUPPORT PLAN

I. INTRODUCTION

Program Name

Brief Description

Launch Date

- Summary

- Definition for Word of Mouth Marketing

II. PLANNING

One: AUDIT

<u>Market Development Checklist</u>

- Situation Analysis

- Target Customer

- Compelling Reason to Buy

- MDSC Checklist

- Whole Product Analysis

- Partners, Allies, Relationships

- Distribution

- Pricing

- Competitive environment

- Positioning relative to TALC

Communications Environment

- Existing Arsenal
- Processes

Two: STRATEGY

Marketing Objectives

- The Challenge
- Growth Strategy
- Additional Growth Areas

Communications Objectives

- Revenue goals, sales requirements.
- Sales support, lead flow requirements
- Long term goals
- Short term goals

Communications Strategies

- Key features & benefits chart
- Product Positioning Chart
- Creative Repository Prelude

Communications Tactics:

Word of Mouth Marketing

- Influencer Relations
- Viral Marketing
- Accelerated Contagion

Three: CREATIVE

- The creative process
- Creative elements
- Positioning
- Exploring a creative platform

III. EXECUTION

One: ARSENAL

- Sales support
- Viral marketing
- Influential relations
- Accelerated contagion

Two: DEPLOYMENT

- Funding and budgets
- Dependencies
- Issues to be resolved
- Basic tactical challenges
- Social Media

Three: TRACKING, TESTING, & KEEPING THE BUZZ ALIVE

- It's hard to get it going, still harder to maintain.
- Focus, test, and believe.
- Technology Adoption Life Cycle.

Why read Embedded Word of Mouth?

Marketers today need to understand how to apply word of mouth marketing, which took off dramatically about 10 years ago, because this is the umbrella concept, or foundation, which spawned social media.

From Pete Blackshaw, author of *Satisfied Customers Tell Three Friends, Angry Customers Tell 3,000*, evolved the concept of CGM (consumer-generated media). To use Pete's words, *"What exactly is CGM? It is the currency of a new commercial relationship between business and consumer. It is the endless stream of comments, opinions, emotions, and personal stories about any and every company, product, service or brand, which consumers can now post online and broadcast to millions of other consumer with the click of the mouse".* Sort of sounds like social media doesn't it?

So now that we see the relationship between word of mouth marketing and social media how do we bundle them with the still-relevant and valuable disciplines of traditional marketing? That's where the marcom engine comes in. It provides a vehicle and a blueprint for blending messaging and media into a viable sales and marketing communications go-to-market strategy.

Get a copy. Share with a friend. Help a marketing buddy bridge the gap between traditional advertising and today's accelerating social media juggernaut. You'll be glad you did.

Keith Bates
keithbates@kbates.com
www.kbates.com
www.keithbatesblog.com

www.ingramcontent.com/pod-product-compliance
Lightning Source LLC
Chambersburg PA
CBHW051521170526
45165CB00002B/561

* 9 7 8 1 4 6 1 1 8 8 3 0 8 *